THE BOOK OF SUFI RIBALDRY

Sana'i, Anvari, Mahsati, Rumi,
Sadi & Obeyd Zakani

For a complete list of our publications

go to the back of this book

THE BOOK OF SUFI RIBALDRY

Sana'i, Anvari, Mahsati, Rumi,
Sadi & Obeyd Zakani

Translations and Introduction

Paul Smith

NEW HUMANITY BOOKS

BOOK HEAVEN
Booksellers & Publishers

NEW HUMANITY BOOKS
BOOK HEAVEN
(Booksellers & Publishers for over 40 years)
47 Main Road
Campbells Creek, Victoria 3451
Australia

www.newhumanitybooks.com

ISBN: 978-1508472612

Poetry/Satire/Ribald Poetry/Sufism/Middle Eastern Studies/
Persian Literature

CONTENTS

Forms in Classical Persian Poetry
Used by our Poets

The Ghazal.

There is really no equivalent to the *ghazal* (pronounced *guz'el*) in English poetry although Masud Farzaad,* perhaps the greatest Iranian authority on Hafiz (he spent much his lifetime finding the Variorum Edition) and his *ghazals* says, the sonnet is probably the closest. As a matter of fact, the *ghazal* is a unique form and its origin has been argued about for many centuries.

Some say that the *ghazal* originated in songs that were composed in Persia to be sung at court before Persia was converted to Islam, but not one song has survived to prove this. It is also possible that originally the *ghazals* were songs of love that were sung by minstrels in the early days of Persian history and that this form passed into poetry down the ages. I find this explanation plausible for the following reasons: firstly, the word *ghazal* means 'a conversation between lovers.' Secondly, the *ghazals* of Hafiz, Sadi and others were often put to music and became songs, which have been popular in Persia from ancient times until now.

Other scholars see the *ghazal* as coming from Arabic poetry, especially the prelude to longer poems: they say that this prelude was isolated and changed, to eventually become the *ghazal*. The Arabic root of the word *ghazal* is *gazl* which means: spinning, spun, thread, twist... the form of the *ghazal* is a spiral.

Whatever the origin, by the fourteenth century the *ghazal* had become a mature form of poetry. Among the great *ghazal* writers in Persian of the past were Nizami, Farid ad-Din 'Attar, Rumi and Sadi; but with the *ghazals* of Hafiz and other poets in Shiraz during his lifetime this form reached its summit.

The form of the *ghazal* at first glance seems simple, but on a deeper inspection it will be found that there is more to it than one at first sees.

It is usually between five and fifteen couplets (*beyts* or 'houses'), but sometimes more. A *beyt* is 'a line of verse split into two equal parts scanning exactly alike.' Each couplet has a fixed rhyme that appears at the end of the second line. In the first couplet that is called the *matla* meaning 'orient' or 'rising,' the rhyme appears at the end of both lines. This first couplet has the function of 'setting the stage' or stating the subject matter and feeling of the poem. The other couplets or *beyts* have other names depending on their positions. One could say that the opening couplet is the subject, the following couplets the actions: changing, viewed from different angles, progressing from one point to another, larger and deeper, until the objective of the poem is reached in the last couplet. The final couplet is known as the *maqta* or 'point of section.' This couplet or the one before it almost always contains the *takhallus* or pen-name of the poet, signifying that it was written by him and also allowing him the chance to detach himself from himself and comment on what effect the actions of the subject matter in the preceding couplets had on him. Often the poet uses a play on words when he uses his own pen-name... ('Hafiz' for example, means: a preserver, a guardian, rememberer, watchman, one who knows the *Koran* by heart. 'Jahan' means: the world).

Hafeez and his Poems by Masud Farzaad. Stephen Austin & Sons Ltd. Hertford, 1949.

The Ruba'i

Many scholars of Persian Poetry believe that the *ruba'i* is the most ancient Persian poetic form that is original to this language and they state that all other classical forms including the *ghazal, qasida, masnavi, qit'a* and others originated in Arabic literature and the metres employed in them were in Arabic poetry in the beginning... this, can be disputed.

The *ruba'i* is a poem of four lines in which usually the first, second and fourth lines rhyme and sometimes with the *radif* (refrain) after the rhyme words... sometimes all four rhyme. It is composed in metres called *ruba'i* metres. Each *ruba'i* is a separate poem in itself and should not be regarded as a part of a long poem as was created by FitzGerald when he translated those he attributed to Omar Khayyam.

The *ruba'i* (as its name implies) is two couplets *(beyts)* in length, or four lines *(misra)*. The *ruba'i* is a different metre from those used in Arabic poetry that preceded it.

How was this metre invented? The accepted story of Rudaki (d. 941) creating this new *metre* of the *hazaj* group which is essential to the *ruba'i* is as follows: one New Year's

Festival *(Nowruz)* he happened to be strolling in a garden where some children played with nuts and one threw a walnut along a groove in a stick and it jumped out then rolled back again creating a sound and the children shouted with delight in imitation, *'Ghaltan ghaltan hami ravad ta bun-i gau,' (Ball, ball, surprising hills to end of a brave try)*. Rudaki immediately recognised in the line's metre a new invention and by the repetition four times of the *rhyme* he had quickly created the *ruba'i*... and is considered the first master of this form and the father of classical Persian Poetry.

Shams-e Qais writing two hundred years later about this moment of poetic history and the effect of this new form on the population said the following... "This new poetic form fascinated all classes, rich and poor, ascetic and drunken rebel-outsider *(rend)*, all wanted to participate in it... the sinful and the good both loved it; those who were so ignorant they couldn't make out the difference between poetry and prose began to dance to it; those with dead hearts who couldn't tell the difference between a donkey braying and reed's wailing and were a thousand miles away from listening to a lute's strumming, offered up their souls for a *ruba'i*. Many young cloistered girls, from passion for the song of a *ruba'i* broke down the doors and their chastity's walls; many matrons from love for a *ruba'i* let loose the braids of their self-restraint."

And so, the *ruba'i* should be eloquent, spontaneous and ingenious. In the *ruba'i* the first three lines serve as an introduction to the fourth that should be sublime, subtle or pithy and clever. As can be seen from the quote by Shams-e Qais above, the *ruba'i* immediately appealed to all levels of society and has done so ever since. The nobility and royalty enjoyed those in praise of them and the commoner enjoyed the short, simple homilies... the ascetic and mystic could think upon epigrams of deep religious fervour and wisdom; the reprobates enjoyed the subtle and amusing satires and obscenities... and for everyone, especially the cloistered girls and old maids, many erotic and beautiful love poems to satisfy any passionate heart.

Almost every major and minor poet in Persia composed at some time in the *ruba'i* form.

The Qasida

This kind of poem resembles a *ghazal* in many ways except that it is longer than the *ghazal* and is often as long as a hundred couplets. In the first couplet, both the lines rhyme, and the same rhyme runs through the whole poem, the rhyme-word being at the end of the second line of each couplet (after the first couplet) as in the *ghazal*. The *qasida* (which means 'purpose') is usually written in praise of someone and is often read in his or her presence, so it is stated that it shouldn't be too long or it might weary the listener. It has a number of sections: i. *matla* - the beginning, ii. *taghazzul* -introduction, iii. *guriz* - the couplets in praise of whoever it is written to, iv. *maqta*- the end. In the *qasida*, the *takhallus* or pen-name of the poet usually does not appear, and if it does it is not necessarily near the end or at the end as in the *ghazal*. Any metre may be used except that used for the *ruba'i* .

The Masnavi

The *masnavi* is the form used in Persian poetry to write epic ballads or romances and is essentially a Persian invention. Each couplet has a different rhyme with both lines rhyming. This is to allow the poet greater freedom to go into a longer description of the subject he has chosen to present. All of the great, long, narrative poems of Persia were composed in this form that is a Persian invention and is not known in classical Arabic poetry. The most famous poems written in this form are the 'Shahnama' (Book of the Kings) of Firdausi, the 'Enclosed Garden of the Truth' of Sana'i, the 'Five Treasures' of Nizami, the 'Conference of the Birds' and 'The Book of God' and so many others by 'Attar, the 'Seven Thrones' of Jami, the ten *masnavis* of Amir Khusraw and of course the great 'Masnavi' of Rumi.

In the 'Book of the Winebringer' *masnavi,* Hafiz uses a device in relation to the *masnavi* form invented by Nizami in his epic poem *Layla & Majnun.* It is an internal rhyme structure in most of the couplets by beginning many of them with "Winebringer, come" or "Give," and produces a kind of chant *(radif)* that is not dissimilar to the repetition of a word or words that he places at the end of many of his *ghazals*.

The Qit'a

The *qit'a* or 'fragment' must consist of at least two couplets and is similar to a *ghazal* or a *qasida* with the second lines of the couplets all having the same rhyme... but in the first couplet the double-rhyme does not usually appear. It can be composed in any metre except for that of the *ruba'i*. It can be a fragment from a *qasida* or a *ghazal*, or it may be complete in itself.

The Tarji-band

This kind of strophe (band) poem consists of a series of stanzas each containing a variable but equal, or nearly equal, number of couplets all in one rhyme, these stanzas being separated from each other by a series of isolated couplets that mark the end of each strophe. If the same couplet (or refrain) is repeated at the end of each *band*, or strophe, the poem is a *tarji-band*, or 'return-tie'.

Sources...

Literary History of Persia Volume 2 by E.G. Browne. Cambridge University Press, 1928. (Pages 22-76).

History of Iranian Literature by Jan Rypka et al. D. Reidel Publishing Company, Dordrecht. 1968. (pages 91-105).

Classical Persian Literature by A.J. Arberry. George Allen & Unwin Ltd. London. 1958. (Pages 1-16).

An Introduction to Persian Literature by Reuben Levy. Columbia University Press, New York, 1969. (Pages 27-44).

SANA'I

A popular and influential poet in the royal court in Ghazneh (in western Afghanistan) during the late 11th and early 12th centuries, Hakim Sana'i (Abu al-Majd Majdud ibn Adam) (1050–1131) is best known for his classic mystical poem in *masnavi* (rhyming couplets) form 'The Enclosed Garden of the Truth and the Law of the Path'. He is considered one of the finest poets in the Sufi (Islamic mysticism) tradition.

He is most commonly referred to as Hakim Sana'i, which he used as his pen-name or *takhallus*. Sana'i means 'insight'. The epithet 'hakim' ('wise one') was typically reserved for people of great learning. However, he is also referred to variously as Madjdud Sana'i, Adam al-Ghaznawi, Adam Sana'i al-Ghaznavi, and simply Sana'i.

Sana'i was born in the city of Ghazneh. Most sources give 1050 as the year of his birth, although, like his name, the date varies somewhat. His father was a teacher, but to what extent and in what disciplines Sana'i himself was educated is uncertain.

As a young man he seems to have had a talent for enlisting the interest and help of potential patrons from all classes of Ghaznian society. There are records of his interactions with state officials, soldiers, Islamic clergymen, scholars, and poets. Perhaps his most important relationships were with several prominent academics from the Hanafi school of law.

Sanai's cultivation of numerous patrons and allies, together with his tremendous talent as a poet, led to his appointment as the official court poet of the sultans of Ghazneh. His panegyrics - the lofty, elaborate writings in which he lavishly praised the rulers - made him the darling of the court. Sana'i appears to have suddenly abandoned his career as a professional poet after making the acquaintance of a 'drinker of dregs' (in modern terms, a drunkard)... a *mast,* or God-intoxicated soul named Lai Khur in about 1114. Whether this person was the reason the poet left his career or not, it is known that Sana'i shortly after left the city of his birth. Records indicate that Sana'i was strongly influenced by the drunkard, who reportedly criticized the poet for writing "in praise of unworthy persons... for worldly gains. What will you say to God on the day of the reckoning when He asks, 'What have you brought for me?' " Upon hearing this Sana'i is said to have immediately left the court's service... gave up writing panegyrics and embarked upon a spiritual journey.

His first stop on his trek was Balkh. From there he reportedly traveled to other cities in Khorasan province, which is now part of Iran. He eventually found his way to Merv in modern Turkmenistan where he dedicated himself to seeking perfection of the soul. He also turned his attention to securing the patronage of the religious class. An influential Hanafi scholar and mystic Shaikh Yusuf Hamadani whose abode was called 'The *Kaaba* of Khorasan', took Sana'i under his wing and became the poet's spiritual Master.

While living in Khorasan he became a highly praised writer of spiritual poetry. Despite his success and popularity in his adopted home however, Sana'i decided, for reasons that remain unclear, to return to his native city of Ghazneh in about 1126. At the time, mystical and religious writing was popular among the ruling classes and the poet soon attracted the attention of the sultan Bahramshah. The sultan quickly became his sole patron, encouraging the aging poet to reside with him at the court. Sana'i resisted, determined to maintain his longtime aloofness from worldly matters, but he wrote and dedicated his most important poem to the sultan, indicating that Bahramshah had a major influence on Sana'i. But the poet did remain in seclusion for the remainder of his life.

For the sultan, the now aged Sana'i wrote the first major *masnavi* (rhymed couplets) in the Dari/Persian language. Titled 'The Enclosed Garden of the Truth and the Law of the Path', the poem contained mystical teachings intermingled with proverbs, fables, and anecdotes. The uncommon manner in which Sana'i introduced and explained the esoteric teachings of Sufism through the medium of poetry was the key to its popularity and lasting value. It is still widely considered by scholars to be the first great mystical poem in Persian and the work had wide-reaching influence on both Muslim and Persian literature. It became a mainstay of study in the Sufi centers of Multan, Delhi, and Gulbarga. Composed of 10,000 couplets, the poem spans ten different sections.

Sana'i was one of the first poets to use the *masnavi* (epic), the *qasida* (ode) and the *ghazal* (lyric) and over 400 *ruba'is* (quatrains) to convey and express the mystical, ethical, and philosophical concepts of Sufism, or Islamic mysticism...

altogether, his collection of poetry or *Divan* comprises about 30,000 couplets. His other known *masnavis* are "Path of Verification', 'Book of the Stranger', 'Pilgrimage of Servants to the Here-after', 'Book of Deeds', 'Book of Love', 'Book of Reason'. All are rare and have not been translated into English.

Despite his vow never to write panegyrics again, the presence of mild praise even in some of the poet's religious works indicates that he depended upon his patrons for material, if not spiritual, support.

Sana'i died in Ghazneh in about 1131. Scholars believe that he was unable to finish 'The Walled Garden of Truth', as we now know it, before his death. Although all couplets are attributed to him, historians believe that substantial editorial work by other poets (perhaps commissioned by Bahramshah) was done to coax the work into its final form. It is said to have had an influence on Rumi in composing his *Masnavi* and Sadi in composing his *Bustan* ('The Orchard'). Rumi said, 'Attar is the soul and Sana'i the eyes, and I came after them'.

The 'ribald' *masnavi* that follows is from 'The Walled garden of the Truth'.

Selected Bibliography

Sana'i: Selected Poetry, Translation & Introduction by Paul Smith, New Humanity Books, Campbells Creek. 2012

Ruba'iyat of Sana'i, Translation & Introduction by Paul Smith, New Humanity Books, Campbells Creek, 2012.

The Enclosed Garden of the Truth by Hakim Abu l-Majd Majdud Sana'i of Ghazneh Edited and translated by Major J. Stephenson. Samuel Weiser, Inc. New York 1968, reprint. (One 6th of the book).

The Walled Garden of Truth, translated and abridged by David Pendlebury, E.P. Dutton, New York, 1976

A Thousand Years of Persian Ruba'iya't by Reza Saberi. Ibex Publishers Maryland, 2000. (Pages 121-142).

Ghazal as World Literature 1: Transformations of a Literary Genre. Edited by Thomas Bauer and Angelika Neuwirth. Orient-Institut, Beirut. 2005. (Pages 327-336).

Of Piety and Poetry: The Interaction of Religion and Literature in the Life and Works of Hakim Sana'i of Ghazna, by J.T.P. de Bruijn, Leiden 1983.

Persian Sufi Poetry: An Introduction to the Mystical Use of Classical Poems, by J.T.P. de Bruijn, Curzon Press, Surrey. 1997. (Pages 35-43, 88-95 et-al).

Development of the Ghazal and Khaqani's Contribution: A Study on the Development of Ghazal and a Literary Exegesis of a 12th c. Poetic Harbinger: A dissertation presented by Alireza Korangy Isfahani. Harvard University 2007. (UMI microform 3265145).

Suppressed Persian. An Anthology of Forbidden Literature. Translated with Notes and an Introduction by Paul Sprachman. Mazda Pub., Costa Mesa, 1995. (Pages 5-13… his 'obscene' poetry).

A Golden Treasury of Persian Poetry by Hadi Hasan, Indian Council for Cultural Relations, New Delhi, 1966. (Pages 94-102).

Literary History of Persia by E.G. Browne, Vol. 2 Cambridge University Press 1928 (Pages 317-322).

Reading, Writing & Recitation: Sana'i and the Origins of the Persian Ghazal, F. Lewis, Ph.D. diss, U. of Chicago, 1995.

Wikipedia article.

GHAZALS...

At morning returning drunk into my lane turned you,
your hair was dishevelled and your face was dirty too.
Due to the dirty face of yours that like the sun shone,
embarrassed the dawn looked away, what I say's true!
And, because of one look from your flirtatious eyes...
wife was left by the husband, husband by wife... too!
Like flooding rain kisses from your lips were flowing
full of joy your lips smiling... teeth showing through,
feeding this hungry heart of mine... from then on my
lips wait, breathless in that lane for a kiss from you!
All of that night and the next day you delighted me
with your face like a fire and curls tangled through...
"O Sana'i, don't take any notice of those hypocrites,
turn your back away, they are not friends, it's true!"

The embrace of whom is the home of all goodness:

prayer-arch of souls on whose shoulder is? Guess!

You are that, which universal mind sees through,

in that centre of your silent ruby is you, to bless!

You, you are that haven for the heavenly sphere,

where it drinks at your fountain of youthfulness!

Lion goes on prowling as gazelles are feasting...

I am... the prey, a dumb rabbit sleeping, no less!

And that scent of linen that nestles in your hair,

puts to shame all the musk... all the ambergris.

That musky armour of yours, that is in a fever...

its chains has got me tangled up, all in a mess!

"Be drinking up," how long will they be saying:

your wine-drinking lips, so full, of sweetness?

You will want me intoxicated for... how long?

Your words I cling to even in my drunkenness!

A hundred or more like me there truly must be,

all who have become bewitched by you, no less.

And, they are hopelessly confused, like I am...

all the world by your eyes, is made senseless.

Sana'i, know that you are a slave, ear-marked,

head over heals in love with this beloved, this

young beloved, Sana'i… will it be do you think

until you're not thought of as forgotten? Guess!

QIT'AS...

(A poem about a 'victim' of Sana'i's humour who wanted to be praised and not have to pay anything)

He believes, poets who praise him while

eating his dinner, should receive no pay;

being so wise and great, of such nobility,

that he can be praised, 'come what may'.

If I praise him, I'll only receive brain-rot;

if critical, this tongue in slime would lay!

To praise such a fat-arsed donkey is a lie:

lampooning a cuckolded fool, is mere play!

[Ali She Buseh was a poet of the time, now unknown, who obviously got on the wrong side of Sana'i... hence the poem below]

Ali Seh Buseh, for you I'll invent a curse,
here is one that your life will spicing up...
in bleeding pussy of a woman your beard,
your mother a donkey's prick be hard up!

The anus of you wife's better-looking than you,

when I look at it with my natural appreciation.

If desires of this man you did not let happen...

I'd do to it, what with you comes satisfaction.

MASNAVI...

About that holy Khwaja of Herat you have heard,

that prodigious Sufi so clever in ways of the word?

The times, the age he lived him tired him so much;

but still, he was the world's wisest man by much!

He was far ahead of all others, due to his brain...

by life's trials and temptations, that was in vain!

Ah no, one thing by which he was set back a peg,

sore had become his growing, middle... third leg!

The last time that he had a fuck was now awhile;

so some boy he got but a spot was not to it defile.

That one became worried as no shelter was there,

then remembered the mosque, vacant, quite near.

Empty was that mosque as was the niche to pray;

so, he thought, "I will get into it, straight away."

Then, when those silver hills of ore he unveiled...

his salmon up-stream he was about to have sped:

suddenly, that mosque was so full of bright light,

as when from coal sparks fly off from pick's might.

Some devotee had seen him going in that place...

and realizing what was happening went in apace.

Like a rope he saw that boy's neck was twisted...

as the other was ready to go in with rod extended:

but before the bum-hole's ring that one did touch,

he charged that pious one who penis he did clutch!

His hand was raised and his fist and his cane too,

opening his mouth like some cow insults he threw:

"All of these sinful ways of yours, I'm telling you,

have brought a drought turned crops into mildew!

How could you such a thing in the house of God?

Once you were God's light, now just a limp rod!

You're just some nothing now, a son of a whore...

in our Islam, such a thing, is something to abhor!

To us has now come time of the Last Judgment...

it is now turn of ignorance to get what is meant!

Of that One the population has no fear anymore:

all desires they have their hearts follow, for *more!*

This land is now stained by your wicked ways...

this land's now in drought, sky knew better days!

There's no greenery now upon the earth's surface,
and all of our people each other they cannot face!
The adulterers and the pederasts are everywhere:
the showers of April have dried up, it is *despair!*
When perverts like you use prayer-niche for lust,
in this age of ours who now can any one trust?"
That 'Khwaja', that 'pervert' now slipped out...
the pious devotee he wished to avoid, no doubt.
When outside of the mosque's door he stepped
that pious one took his place... to spot rooted.
Then, when that 'pervert' looked inside again,
he saw that foe at it like he had... once again!
He could see that the old hypocrite was at it...
his old carrot was working hard, not a tight fit!
Inside that door he poked his head and shouted:
"Mosques the same as is the act, hey dickhead?
My luck is like this I guess I have to accept it:
what for you is allowed for me isn't, damn it!"
May exultation of the Almighty be boundless,
the ways of these times have changed, no less!

Upon all the earth the crops again are growing,

and the people have strength to again be living.

My God's grace not diminish, thank the Lord:

instead of the rain clouds send pearls to hoard!

To those empty clouds new rain has arrived…

all the people now truly cry, joyfully out loud!

In the fields is a life now, with more to give…

all in the world now get on with trying to live!

O all of you really pious souls worth so much,

to this earth only you bring that worthy touch.

Of course, you have the true view of Paradise,

because of that… our Islam is from your eyes!

If this dick-head is like the world's dick-heads,

one can't expect more… from other dick-heads!

Listen to this, if this is how such a one's acting,

towards his neighborhood, you, never be going!

And if this is what a Sufi refers to as an 'easy',

let prick big as the world be up his wife's pussy.

ANVARI

Ahad-ud-din Anvari Abeverdi (1126-1189) was a court poet of the Seljuk sultans. Jami composed a *ruba'i* where he names him, along with Firdausi and Sadi as one of the 'three prophets' of Persian poetry...

> *Three people are prophets in poetry:*
> *all men upon this statement agree...*
> *Firdausi and Anvari, and also Sadi,*
> *although... 'No prophets, after me!'*

He was mainly a court poet of Sultan Sanjar (although he praised 66 patrons in all)... he was also a celebrated astronomer, mathematician and scientist who admitted he gave them up for the more lucrative occupation of being... a court poet, that he later rejected twenty years before his death for a life of seclusion and contemplation.

He is renowned for his delightful wittiness that can be found in many of his *ruba'is* and *qit'as and ghazals*. He is one of the greatest Persian masters of the *qasida* and his one that has been called 'The Tears of Khurasan' is considered to be one of his masterpieces. He created a new style of poetry by using the conversational language of his time in clear and simple words and expressions, sometimes quite down to earth. He was greatly influenced by Arab poets of the *qasida,* in particular Imra' ul-Qays and al-Mutanabbi. (See their *qasidas* in my 'The Qasida: A World Anthology').

Jan Rypka (see forthcoming) states, "Thanks to his imagination, learning and sovereign mastery of language and rhetoric, he raised the *qasida* to such a high level that a subsequent decline was inevitable. Jami speaks of him as 'almost a miracle' and is also right in another sense than he meant, for with all his linguistic peculiarities and Arabisms Anvari is a master of *sahl-i mumtany',* if one interprets this professional term here as the 'inimitable facility' with which he composed his verse. He often begins his *qasida* immediately with a eulogy, while descriptions of nature are only seldom to be found in the introductions; there is no excess or eroticism but on the other hand the dialogues with the Beloved, i.e. the object of his praise, are striking. In his pleadings he likes to include a touch of humour, a characteristic feature of his *qasidas.*"

He is known for his sense of humour and sometimes even obscenity that can be found in many of his *qit'as...* (see forthcoming).

He created a new style of poetry by using the conversational language of his time in clear and simple words and expressions.

Selected Bibliography

Kulliyat (Collected Works) Anvari. Lucknow, 1880.

Anvari: Selected Poems, Translation & introduction, Paul Smith, New Humanity Books, Campbells Creek. 2012.

Ruba'iyat of Anvari, Translation & Introduction by Paul smith, New Humanity Books, 2012.

A Thousand Years of Persian Ruba'iya't by Reza Saberi. Ibex Publishers Maryland, 2000. (Pages 195-204).

The Life & Works of Hakim Auhad-ud-din Anwari by Dr. K.B. Nasim, University of Panjab, Lahore, 1965. (A wonderful book)

Anwari: Material for a Biography and Characteristic Sketch by V. A. Zhukovski, St. Petersburg, 1883.

Studies on the Poetry of Anvari ed. by Daniela Meneghins, Eurasiatica, Venice, 2006.

A Literary History of Persia Vol 2 By Edward G. Browne. Cambridge University Press, London 1902. (Pages 364-390)

An Introduction to Persian Literature by Reuben Levy Columbia University Press 1969 (Pages 148-150)

Islamic Poetry and Mysticism. R.A. Nicholson. Cambridge University Press. 1921.

An Invitation to Persian Poetry, Translated from the Persian by Reza Saberi. Ketab Corp., Los Angeles, 2006. (Pages 105-9).

A Golden Treasury of Persian Poetry by Hadi Hasan. Indian Council for Cultural Relations. Bombay. 1966. (Pages 102-110)

Borrowed Ware. Medieval Persian Epigrams Translated by Dick Davis Mage Pub. Washington DC 1997 (Pages 96-103)

Music of a Distant Drum. Translated and Introduced by Bernard Lewis. Princeton University Press 2001 (Pages 107-9)

Persian Poems Ed. by A.J. Arberry. Dent 1954 (Pages 101-6)

Classical Persian Literature by A.J. Arberry. George Allen & Unwin, London 1958 (Pages 115-119)

Suppressed Persian. An Anthology of Forbidden Literature. Translated with Notes and an Introduction by Paul Sprachman. Mazda Pub., Costa Mesa, 1995. (Pages 14-18).

The Beharistan (Abode of Spring) By Jami. English Translation from the Persian by Edward Rehatsek. Kama Shastra Society, Benares, 1887. (Pages 147-8).

QASIDA...

(In the following poem, a *qasida,* one of Anvari's satires or
'obscene' poems, the title of 'Khwaja' means 'Kind Sir' or
someone from the upper class or aristocracy or clergy...
a so-called 'respectable' member of the community)

If Kind Sir decides to come to me, full of humility,
and should do me the honour today of visiting me,
there would never be any obligation, that I swear...
our love of this life, would so greatly increased be!
We're here, with wine and soup tasting wonderful;
and... a young minstrel who can play wonderfully:
there is one who is already strumming on the lute,
while sweetly singing love and folk songs quietly.
And winebringer worth embracing, shy and slim:
such a boy as that no *huri** ever birthed... to see!
That one alone knows how kind sirs are serviced:
that one's used to clothes to sleep in, intimately.

If, Kind Sir should desire something, different...
I could show that one a way to children, secretly.
But, if you wish to be knocking on another door,
our friendly whores Kind Sir can visit... quietly.
Available for you is this small, fascinating girl
who's so clever even a *huri* would entranced be:
and if you fuck her good just once you'll go mad
from desire, lips chafing, teeth grinding madly.
Kind Sir, let's imagine you've some other taste,
inclining to someone's small daughter you see;
we know a girl for you who is pure, untouched,
who's such no fairy created one of such purity.
Your name would never be asked, no gossip...
all that one would do is remove pants, slowly.
But... if Kind Sir like a famous poet or writer,
finds girls both young and older 'not for me',
I have our pride and glory, a handsome boy...
who can fill you up with a large suppository.
A donkey would envy his width and length,
Kind Sir would find his size... ah, so tasty.

Prick, pussy, anus we have... you are lucky:

you can let them go... or fuck all separately!

I have now said it all, that is all available...

all Kind Sir has to do is call, it's that easy!

QIT'AS...

I composed a eulogy about you, and I regret it...
is there a point in poetry only one has created?
The praise I gave you was like a wet dream and
on waking I saw I had worthlessly... ejaculated.

Since I was unveiling the pussy of your fame,
arsehole of my mind is ripped... I'm stuffed!
If without generous prick you don't fuck me,
your balls with my invective will be crushed!

When, one has the urge a shit to be having

one has a shit, nothing one can do… but it!

Believe what I say, as I've put it to the test:

nothing else will do… but a really good shit.

We've often farted and stunk the place out,

but nothing else works… you can't beat it!

MAHSATI

We know very little of Manisa Mahsati (mah... 'moon', sati... 'lady') Ganjavi's life except that she lived in Ganjeh where Sultan Sanjar reigned (1117-57) and as she was a poet, singer, musician and chess-player at his court she would have known Anvari and other poets there. It is said that her father was a theologian of the city of Khujand and she was born there in 1098 and that after her father's death she and her mother went to Ganjeh where they were finally given a room in a brothel.

She was a court, dervish and ribald poet (perhaps due to her accommodation as a child). She knew Nizami and is said to have been buried in his mausoleum, having died in 1185... although he did not pass away until 1209, 24 years later! She also knew Omar Khayyam, and like Omar composed mainly in the *ruba'i* form and must be considered to have helped revolutionize it. She did compose a few *qit'as* (fragments) such as the following that have come down to us...

Do you want to unite with me?
You hold onto a useless desire!
One cannot even dream of it...

why hold to this useless desire?

Where's breeze one can't access:

can anyone ever win one's desire?

And another...

Would to God that I was that one's thumb-stall,

so on his thumb I might pine away, beyond recall;

whenever he would be shooting that arrow of his

I'd make sure I would myself by it suffer... thrall.

And, when that one would fasten me, O so right,

from that one's lips to grab some kisses, I'd stall.

It is stated that Mahsati composed this poem while watching a Turkish boy shooting arrows. It happened that his thumb-stall over-turned and he fastened it with his teeth.

She was also a great *ghazal* poet but few have come down to us. Alireza Korangy Isfahani (see following) states: 'Mahasti Ganjavi is without a doubt one of the greatest *ghazal* poets of the twelfth century... her flow of ideas is very much akin to the kind of composition we find in the *ghazals* of Hafiz and Sa'di.'

A rare example of one of her *ghazals*...

With this sorrowful heart of mine in tears constantly I am;

like the flute, used to own moaning its easy to see... I am.

Other than my two old companions, agony and affliction:
I've no other as friend in this place where inevitably I am.
Who am I? A madwoman whose soul, heart wants pain...
and thinks that death will my ultimate comfort be... I am.
At companions' feet I'm candle burning... I burn, so I live:
beyond that flame that flickers, my last days to see, I am.
Like that bubble I am that all of its life was able to survive
because like it knowing my foundation is water only, I am.
I'm a rosebud withered away that in spring lost its beauty:
my youth's a rose blown away by the wind, memory I am.
It's only for death that to the Almighty I'm praying often:
this is the only thing that looking forward to happily, I am.
For Mahasti no candle like a companion has been found...
would anyone come and mourn me when dead finally I am?

She was a strong influence on perhaps Persia's greatest female poet Jahan Khatun of Shiraz and Persia's greatest satirist Obeyd Zakani. She was famous and also infamous for her liberated behaviour. She is said to have had many affairs, also with the sultan who found her of interest when after he was about to mount his horse discovered a sudden fall of snow had covered the field and she composed for him the following *ruba'i* on the spot...

For you... Heaven has saddled Fortune's steed

O sultan... and chosen you from all who lead:

now it spreads a silver sheet upon the ground,

steed's gold-shod hooves... mud won't impede.

'Attar, in his masterpiece epic poem of mystical stories of desperate lovers of God, the *Ilahi-nama (Book of God)* that influenced Maulana Rumi to compose his epic *Masnavi* tells the story of her and Sultan Sanjar...

Mahsati the female poet, who was essentially pure, was a favourite of Sanjar...

and even though her face was not moonlike, still the king was very fond of her.

She was in the Radkan meadow one night when Khusrau-like Sanjar retired,

and Mahsati left the king and towards her own tent she then went, to bed.

Now, Sultan Sanjar had a slave, a winebringer perfect in charm and beauty,

and he would often enjoy both of these qualities, that in that one he did see.

Like a hundred others he loved Mahsati's rival, handsome as is the moon:

Sanjar woke up! Not seeing him he went looking for that ruby-lipped one.

Throwing on a nightgown and in anger taking up a sword of Indian make

he entered his tent to find Mahsati beside him, lovingly... in give and take.

She kept singing these words as she was playing the haunting melody:

"I'll embrace you beside the meadow, although tonight with another I'll be!"

Seeing the situation, Sanjar... remembering her words, to himself said this:

"If I rush in with sword I'll scare them to death and both I'll terribly miss!"

Embarrassed, he finally rushed off and went immediately into his own tent,

and after ten days had passed he prepared a great feast, an illuminating event!

Before Sultan Sanjar, Mahsati played her harp, in a very high-pitched sound...

that winebringer was standing near, a cup in hand, eyes upon the ground.

Quoting the line he heard the other night Sanjar casually asked her to sing it:

when Mahsati heard the king she dropped harp from her lap where it did sit!

She started trembling like a leaf, she swooned, her senses caught in a snare;

the king went to sit by her pillow, sprinkled rosewater on her face and hair.

When finally she was conscious again... her fear returned of Sultan Sanjar,

after ten times fainting and recovering she still couldn't lose her great fear.

Then the king said, "If you're afraid of me, your life's safe, you're your enemy."

She said, "I don't fear that, but this: one night I practiced that line continually,

all night through I repeated it... sometimes I liked it, sometimes I did not:

now I am reminded of that night and the world is closing around me like a knot.

It seems that one night while I was doing this, you were secretly watching me:

if you seize me or send me away your heart will revolt and back... be calling me.

And even if you should go and be killing me while I am still a healthy woman...

all you would really be doing would be only freeing me from existence's prison!

The reason I'm so afraid is because that King Who is the world's supporter

is with me each moment of my life and sees every moment that I'm the doer!

And if God that Almighty King happens to confront me with all of my

secret thoughts of say... a hundred years, then what shall I do or say, or try?"

As God sees one always, both night and day; be happy, and smile while

like a candle, you are burning and do not breathe a single breath... while

you're not thanking Him... and do no not breathe a breath in forgetfulness:

if you try to thank Him you will receive reward from His Bountifulness.

She finally married (some say was the mistress of) a son of a preacher, the poet Taju'd-din Amir Ahmad and she found little satisfaction in their torrid relationship and so composed among others (see following) the following ruba'i...

I'm Mahsati and I'm most fair of those to be had:
I am famous for my beauty from Irak to Meshad.
Preacher's boy, you're nothing but useless... bad:
if I get no bread, meat or prick, I get really mad!

Her husband's reply was said to have been...

My prick does not always do what I tell it to:
it's not like your pussy... taking anyone's too!
Weaving a sack out of wool any idiot can do...
but, wind will heighten a tower... is that true?

Her purported love affairs are told in the works of Jauhari of Bukhara. After nearly 900 years, Mahsati is highly respected for her courageous poetry that condemned religious fanaticism and prejudices, hypocrisy and dogmas.

In the city of Ganjeh in Azerbaijan, a street and a school, an academic institution, a museum and others have been named after her. A monument to her was erected in Ganjeh in 1980.

Selected Bibliography

Divan-i Mahsati Ganjavi, Edited by Tahiri Sharab, Ibn Sina, Tehran, 1347 A.H.

Ruba'iyat of Mahsati, Translation & Introduction by Paul Smith, New Humanity Books, Campbells Creek, 2012.

A Thousand Years of Persian Ruba'iya't by Reza Saberi. Ibex Publishers Maryland 2000. (Pages 158-170).

Princesses, Sufis, Dervishes, Martyrs & Feminists: Nine Great Women Poets of the East. Translations, Introduction & Notes by Paul Smith, New Humanity Books, Campbells Creek, 2012.

The Ilahi-nama or Book of God of Farid al-Din 'Attar Translated from the Persian by John Andrew Boyle, Manchester University Press, 1976 (Pages 218-20, 375).

Four Eminent Poetesses of Iran: by M. Ishaque. Iran Society, Calcutta, 1950. (Pages 9-28).

Piercing Pearls: The Complete Anthology of Classical Persian Poetry: Volume One Translations & Introduction by Paul Smith, New Humanity Books, Campbell's Creek. 2008.

Suppressed Persian. An Anthology of Forbidden Literature. Paul Sprachman. Mazda Publications 1995. (Pages 1-5, 8, 61).

A Literary History of Persia Vol 1 From the Earliest Times to Firdawsi By Edward G. Browne. London 1902. (Page 344).

History of Iranian Literature by Jan Rypka et al. D. Reidel Publishing Company Holland. 1968 (Page 199).

Borrowed Ware: Medieval Persian Epigrams, Translated by Dick Davis. Mage Publishers, 1997. (Pages 105-107).

Le Luna e te perle (The moon and the pearls) Italian Translation of her poems by R. Bargigli, D. Meneghini, Ariel Pub. 1999.

Nozhat al-Majalas (Joy of Gatherings) A collection of 4100 ruba'is, 60 by Mahsati. Compiled Shirvani in the 13th c. Tehran, 1987.

Azerbaijanian Poetry, Classic, Modern, Traditional... Edited by Mirza Ibrahimov, Progress Publishers, Moscow, 1969. (Pages 43-47 Trans. by Gladys Evans).

RUBA'IS...

A mine of rubies... a hiding place, the pussy

is:

it, for you a place to rest, a silver pillow settee

is.

Nine months gone... quicksilver sperm left in it

is sprouting a moon that full of a face, lovely,

is!

As his wife was pregnant a judge was shouting,
crying:
he said aloud and out of spite… "What is really
happening?
I'm old… prick's head hasn't in ages been raided:
my whore is no Mary… who caused her to be
showing?"

To that blood-letter, that Jew who is faithless,

with a dull tongue but knife, a killer, no less…

I said, "Open me up, no less than my pussy:"

but he cut wider than his wife's arse, a mess!

That butcher boy, as is his usual way of doing

it,

threw me down, killed me, said, "I'm having

it!"

Then as an apology, he puts his head on my feet:

this, is to blow air under my skin, to be flaying

it.

*Note: This describes a method of skinning goats and sheep by butchers.
This poem is also attributed to the great Sufi poet
Sana'i who died in 1131 and would have met her at court when
she was 33 and would have been a big influence on her.
He also composed ribald ruba'is. See his section.

I discovered that one, lying drunk... upon the

way:

I fell at that one's feet; that hand in mine I did

lay.

That one does not remember any bit of this...

that is, I don't remember but that one does,

today.

To be a winehouse regular and a *kalandar*,*

lover too:

being in a gang of friendly *rends*... drunken

outsider too,

to be one who is infamous before creation...

Creator too:

is, than wearing any hypocrite's cloak... far

better, too.

*Note: Kalandars are lovers of God who have given up attachment to desires
and live only for God. The name comes from a Master named Kalandar
Yusuf. The word means 'pure gold.'
Kalandars are continually on the move and care nothing for their
own condition, as they are only concerned with praising God.

You are a butcher to me, while in your love, burning

am I;

that your knife may reach these very bones... trying

am I.

Your practice is to sell whatever you have butchered...

heaven's sake, if me you kill, don't sell me: begging,

am I!

To be sucking your ruby lips, forever,

I am longing,

to with you take wine in sips, forever,

I am longing.

Whether intoxicated, mad or sober… to

hear harp from your fingertips forever

I am longing.

You are a butcher to me, while in your love, burning

am I;

that your knife may reach these very bones… trying

am I.

Your practice is to sell whatever you've butchered…

heaven's sake, if me you kill, don't sell me: begging,

am I!

Like a horse you gallop sprightly, in the field of

joy…

with subtle ingenuity you do wonders, not being

coy;

with queen, king, pawns, clergy, castles, knights

you play excellently and elegantly, skilfully, my

boy.

RUMI

Jalal-ud-din Rumi was born in 1207 in Balkh. This city was then in the Persian province of Khorasan but is now in Afghanistan. Balkh was a prominent city at that time and his family had a tradition of service there in both legal and religious offices. Despite this he moved when about eleven with his family away from Balkh so as to avoid the warlike Mongols. They travelled to Baghdad, to Mecca on pilgrimage, to Damascus and eventually settled near Konya in what is now western Turkey.

On the road to Anatolia, Jalal-ud-din and his father had encountered one of the most famous mystic Persian poets, Farid ad-din Attar, in the city of Nishapur. Attar immediately recognized the boy's spiritual status. He saw Baha-ud-din, walking ahead of his son and said, "Here comes a sea followed by an ocean." He gave Jalal-ud-din his *Illahi-nama*, 'Book of God'. This meeting had a deep impact on Rumi's thoughts, which later on became the inspiration for his masterpiece *Masnavi*.

Baha-ud-din became the head of a *madrassa* (religious college) and when he died Rumi succeeded him at the age of twenty-five. He married and had two sons. One of Baha-ud-din's students, Syed Burhan-ud-din, continued to train Rumi in the religious and mystical doctrines of Rumi's father. For nine years, Rumi practiced Sufism as a disciple of Burhan-ud-din until Burhan-ud-din died in 1240. During this period Rumi travelled to Damascus and is said to have spent four years there. While there he first caught a glimpse of the *Qutub* (Perfect Master) Shams-e Tabriz clothed in his black-felt cap. Shams called out to him but he turned away and mixed in with the crowd in the market. On returning to Konya Rumi fasted for three consecutive periods of forty days under the guidance of Burhan-ud-din. He pronounced that he had taught Rumi all he could of all sciences, human and spiritual.

In 1244 the perfected dervish Shams-e Tabriz arrived in Konya. This great Spiritual Master, a basket-maker by trade had travelled much in search of other great souls. He went to an inn in Konya under the disguise of a merchant where he began fasting on and off. One day as he sat near the inn's gate Rumi rode up on a mule followed by a large crowd of his many students and disciples on foot. Shams stood then walked over to him and took hold of the mule's bridle and halted the animal and after paying due reverence to the great teacher asked Rumi the following question, "Was Mohammed the greater servant of God, or Bayzid of Bistam?"

Rumi answered, "Incomparably, Mohammed was the greater… the greatest of all the prophets and saints!"

Shams then asked, "Why is it then that Mohammed said, 'We haven't known You God as You should rightly be known' while Bayzid declared, 'Glory be to me! How very great is my glory!'?"

With this Shams had revealed his state of being *Qutub* or Perfect Master to Rumi.

Rumi fainted. On recovering consciousness he asked Shams to come home with him where they were closeted together for weeks and then months and then years in spiritual communication. Four years later on the night of the fifth of December 1248, as Rumi and Shams were talking, Shams was called to the back door. He went out, never to be seen again. It is believed that he was murdered with the help of one of Rumi's sons, Allaedin… Rumi's students and followers had become frustrated and jealous with Shams taking up all the time of their teacher.

Rumi's love and his great longing for Shams, whom he went searching for in Damascus and elsewhere, found expression in music, dance, songs and poems in his collection of poems/songs or *Divan* which he named after his Master... *Divan of Shams-e Tabriz.* This vast work included thousands of *ghazals* and other poetic forms and nearly two thousand *ruba'is* which he would compose for many years, before he became a God-realized Perfect Master himself, and also afterwards.

After 1249 the Seljuk governors paid tribute to the Mongol empire. As vassal of the Mongol Baiju, Mu'in al-Din governed Rum for twenty years starting in 1256, and he patronized Rumi. His disciple Hesam'odin Hasan urged Rumi to write the 'Masnavi' in the style of Sana'i and 'Attar. Rumi completed six books of these before he died on December 17, 1273. In the fifth book are many of the 'ribald stories' he told to get across certain moral and spiritual truths (see below).

Many of his talks were written in the book *Fihi ma fihi,* "In it what is in it" and is often referred to as his 'Discourses'.

Selected Bibliography

Ruba'iyat of Rumi Translation & Introduction by Paul Smith, New Humanity Books, Campbells Creek, 2008.

Rumi: Selections from his Masnavi, Translation & Introduction by Paul Smith, New Humanity Books, Campbells Creek, 2012.

Rumi: Selected Poems, Translation & Introduction by Paul Smith, New Humanity Books, Campbells Creek, 2012.

The Quatrains of Rumi: Translated by Ibrahim W. Gamard and A.G. Rawan Farhadi. Sufi-Dari Books, 2008.

The Ruba'iyat of Jalal al-din Rumi: Select translations into English Verse by A.J. Arberry. Emery Walker, Ltd. London 1949.

Mystical Poems of Rumi... First Selection, Poems 1-200. Translated from the Persian by A.J. Arberry The University of Chicago Press. 1968. (200 of his ghazals in literal trans.).

Mystical Poems of Rumi... Second Selection, Poems 201-400. Translated by A.J. Arberry. Westview Press, Boulder Colorado. 1979. (200 more of his many ghazals in literal trans.)

Divan-i Kebir: Mevlana Celaleddin Rumi. Translated by Nevit O. Ergin from the Turkish translations. Echo Publications, California 22 vols. 1995-2003. (All of his poems... ghazals etc., except his masnavi... in literal trans.)

The Masnavi: Jalal al-din-Rumi, Books One & Two Translated with an Introduction & notes by Jawid Mojaddedi, Oxford University Press, 2004. (A wonderful Trans. of the 1st two books in the correct rhyme... more to come I hope).

The Mathnawi of Jalalu'ddin Rumi Edited from the oldest manuscripts available: with critical notes, translation, & commentary by Reynold A. Nicholson 8 vols. Luzac & Co. London 1926. (The recognized literal trans., but has recently come under much criticism by good scholars for his excluding many true couplets and his mistranslation of key words. Nicholson used Latin when translating Rumi's 'ribald' stories.)

Maulana Rumi's Masnawi Translation and commentary by M.G. Gupta. 6 vols. MG Publishers Agra. 1990.

The Mesnevi of Mevlana (Our Lord) Jelal-ud-din, Muhammad, Er-Rumi. Book the First: Together with some account of The Life and

Acts of the Author, of his Ancestors, and of his descendants, by Mevlana Shems-ud-din Ahmed, El Eflaki, El Arifi Translated by James W. Redhouse. Trubner & Co. London *1881*

Discourses of Rumi... Translated by A.J. Arberry. John Murray, London. *1961.*

Rumi. Past and Present, East and West. The Life, Teaching and Poetry of Jalal al-Din Rumi. Franklin D. Lewis Oneworld Publications Oxford *2000.*

Me & Rumi: The Autobiography of Shams-i Tabrizi Translated, Introduced and Annotated by William C. Chittick, Fons Vitae, Louisville, *2004.* (It should have been called as it was in the Persian 'Discourses of)'.

I Am Wind You Are Fire: The Life and Work of Rumi. Annemarie Schimmel, Shambhala Publications Boston. *1992*

MASNAVIS...

(From volume 5 of Rumi's 'Masnavi'... an example of how sometimes he like Sadi and others used ribald stories to make a point. In this story the king of Mosul surrenders a beautiful girl to the caliph of Egypt who has seen a picture of her and wants her, so that no more Muslim blood will flow if the caliph's massive army invades the city to try to take her by force... but the caliph had not countered on his army's captain falling under her powerful charms and her... surrendering under the captain's powerful... arms. While telling this story Rumi is also explaining why and how the creation came into being... through Love, with a capital 'L'; evolution... through love with a small 'l', and in the end... incarnation of the human being, possibly even re-incarnation, through... 'lovemaking')

When that king's envoy came to that caliph's captain,
he showed the girl's image as the captain did exclaim:
"Look upon this paper and you will see what I require;
listen, we'll conquer you all, if you refuse this desire!"
On his return the envoy was told by his upright king:
"Quickly take her at once, the form means… nothing.
Idol should be with an idol-worshipper, not with me…
I am not of that belief, true worship is never idolatry!"
That envoy then found her, to the captain he took her:
her beauty quickly caught the captain, he… loved her.
Love is an ocean, on which the heavens are mere foam,
like Zulaikha so desiring Joseph comes into her home.
Understand that the heavens turn by wheels of Love,
the world would become frozen if it was not, for Love!
How then would the inorganic ever become… a plant?
How would vegetables sacrifice for a spirit implant?
How would spirit sacrifice itself for sake of a Breath,
by which pure Mary was impregnated, on this earth?
Every single object would become like ice is… fixed:
could they like locusts move, seeking to feed or be fed?

Each mote, each atom is in love with that Perfect All:
each is moving upwards, like a sapling, growing tall.
Their rushing proclaims... "Glory to the Almighty!"
For the sake of their souls they are purifying the body.
The captain believed what was a pit, was a safe road:
that soil to him looked fine, so his seed in it he sowed:
while sleeping, into his dreams had came a vision...
he coupled with that form, greatly flowed his semen!
After the vision disappeared he woke up immediately
and went out and saw that beauty still asleep did be.
He cried, "No, so much precious fluid I have wasted,
I've fallen in love with this one... I've been charmed!"
This captain, this hero... he was not really such a one
to plant his manly seed only in land that was barren.
The steed of his passion champed at a hundred bits...
while he kept on shouting, "What care I, if I die, it's
nothing to me, one in love, if the caliph should kill me,
for one in love, both life and death have, an equality!"
Please, much less passion, do not blow out such heat:
go...talk with a master, get advice from the discreet!

But, what power has advice and reason when desire's

flood has talons sharpened... to destroy greed's fires?

With a barrier in front and a barrier behind... that one

fascinated by lovely cheeks will notice... neither one!

That black torrent will finally come to steal his life...

so that fox will throw that lion into the well of strife!

An illusion is causing to appear in a well, a phantom;

so that it may cast into it, lions strong as a mountain.

Do not let a man and any of your women to get close,

compared to cotton and fire could be the two of those.

Fire would be created only quenched by God's water,

one that like Joseph will not be tempted... no matter

that the charming, supple, cypress-statured Zulaikha

was there, with a lion's will he did withdrew from her.

He turned away from Mosul and he went on his way,

on reaching some woods, they camped later that day.

The fire of that captain's passion was blazing so high

that he couldn't tell if it was day or night by the sky.

He wanted to rush to her in her tent and embrace her:

where had all reason fled to and of the caliph his fear?

When in a wood like this, lust's drum begins to beat!

What does reason become? A radish-top, unfit to eat!

To that one with such fire of desire raging in his eye,

one hundred caliphs right then were less than one fly.

He tore off his trousers: soon he was enthusiastically

exploring the entrance between her thighs, urgently.

When his erect penis headed for her dark secret place,

the army rose up as one and shouted... ready to race

into battle he leapt up and off with backside bare he

led off with that fiery sword in hand... a sight to see!

Coming out of the jungle a fierce black lion he did see

and suddenly it moved into the middle of that army!

All of the Arabian stallions became excited and mad:

each stable and tent many worries had, and all... bad!

That fierce lion from its lair arched, it must have been

twenty feet like billow of a sea, something to be seen!

But that captain was manful, an intrepid man was he:

like a beast at the lion he went... somewhat furiously!

With his sword he struck it... cut deep into its head,

then hurried on back to his tent, to that beauty in bed.

When he showed himself to that crescent of that *huri*,

his penis was seen to be still fully erect, a sight to see!

All the time that he had made combat with that lion

his penis remained at full alert, to droop... not a sign!

That one who was such a sweet picture of loveliness

was full of amazement at the captain's powerfulness:

without wasting another moment, she, out of desire

clung to him, and two souls in one body met, on fire!

Through the union of these two souls with each other,

will come to them from the Unseen, a soul... another!

[From book five of the 'Masnavi'... the story of the female servant who would satisfy her desire with an ass and her mistress who taught the ass to have sexual intercourse like a man... etc.]

A particular female servant from agony due to desire,

took an ass on herself... so as to satisfy her lust's fire.

From her lust that ass became addicted to copulation,

so, it with any woman became addicted to copulation.

That trickster had had devised a way with a pumpkin:

she'd place on his prick... so it would not go too far in.

That ugly woman, when he was about to be entering,

whipped out the pumpkin and then half was entering.

If all the prick of that ass was into her go completely,

her uterus and viscera would've been torn, obviously!

That ass became tired... its mistress, worried, asked:

"Why has my ass become hair-thin, so... exhausted?"

To a farrier she brought the ass and she was asking,

"What's wrong with my ass that it's weight losing?"

He could see nothing wrong with him on the outside
and not a one gave him information about the inside.
She decided to take her investigation more seriously,
and each moment she searched for what it could be.
One's soul has to become devoted to real endeavour
for the seeker becomes the finder by true endeavour.
Then when she was state of that ass investigating,
she saw her narcissus-like, under the ass thrusting.
Through an opening in the door she could see it all,
the old mistress was fascinated, she it did enthrall.
She thought, 'He is having sex with her like a man
just the same as a man has sex… with a woman!'
She was immediately envious, and said… "If, it is
possible, I own the ass, so my right it certainly is!"
That ass, has been totally trained and instructed…
the table is laid out… and the lamp is now lighted!
As if seeing nothing she knocks upon stable's door:
"O maid, how long will you sweep stable's floor?"
As if she knew nothing of what was going on she
called out… "Open this door I am here, it is me!"

Then she was silent, to her maid she didn't talk:
it was her own lust... that forced her not to talk!
Quickly, her servant covered her organ of lustful
obsession and she opened the door quite forceful.
She made her face look sick and her eyes wet too,
and lips together as if to say, "I am fasting, too!"
A soft broom was in her hand as though to say...
"I was sweeping the stable, it's been a hard day!"
When she opened with broom in hand that door,
 her mistress said to herself, "Clever one, before
you made your face look sick, took broom to hand
what reason's for my ass to be thin, I understand.
Halfway through fucking you he was so agitated:
I saw his wet eyes, prick shaking... not satisfied."
She muttered under her breath so she didn't hear:
treating her maid like an innocent... in the clear!
Then, she said to her, "On your head a veil place
and go take a message to such and such a place."
She then asked her to say this and to say that...
all this I have shortened, that woman said that.

Understand the substance of what I'm saying…
that tactful woman her maid was dispatching…
she bolted the door, so happy in her lustfulness
she announced to herself… "Ah, alone I confess
that I shout out in giving thanks… as I am now
delivered from all worry and frustration… now!"
Her hunger, her desire, multiplied a thousand…
as her lust, ran between her thighs… like sand!
Lust, deluded her into thinking she was an owl:
it is some miracle to make an idiot, into an owl.
Lust makes the heart deaf and dumb, not right:
so that an ass looks like Joseph, fire… like light!
So many were intoxicated by fire… by seeking
fire themselves as the Divine light were seeing.
Unless that one is God's devotee, or, is pulled
by God… is led into the way and is changed…
so such a one will know that the light's unreal,
path for such a one is unreal and cannot be real.
The greed of lust makes what is foul seem fair,
and along the path lust's the worst, so beware.

Millions of good names by it were disgraced...
millions of clever humans by it were stupefied!
As it has caused like Joseph an ass to appear...
how will that moron lust, make Joseph appear?
Its spell caused shit to look to you like honey...
when the contest begins what will be... honey?
From eating and drinking too much lust comes;
eat less, or marry and from lust freedom comes.
If you eat and drink, or do what is forbidden...
then you'll discover your income, has all gone.
Marriage is like: 'Without God is no power or
strength', unless the Devil, has all the power!
If, you love eating and drinking, marry soon...
or cat will carry off sheep's tail now, not soon.
As soon as you can place your heavy load upon
your ass, so that you are not soon... put down!
If you don't know effect fire has on you... to go
near fire with no knowledge, is not what to do.
If you have no knowledge of cooking pot and fire,
the pot and soup won't be spared of your desire.

Water must be in it and one has to have skill too
so that the pot is boiled properly… cooking, too.
If you do not understand the blacksmith's way…
near forge you hair and beard will be burnt away.
She locked the door from the inside… she pulled
that ass to her and the bitter aftermath… tasted.
She dragged him into the centre of the room, then
lay on the bench as the maid did, as she had seen.
The excited ass lunged his prick into her as far as
his balls, she died instantly from depth of the ass!
Her liver burst from wound prick of ass inflicted…
one from the other, her intestines were separated!
On side the bench he fell down, she on the other,
her breathing stopped and she gave up the 'other'.
That floor of that stable was with blood covered…
and the woman fell down on her face, she perished.
Her life, had been taken by Time's catastrophe…
O father, martyred by dick of an ass, a possibility?
Listen to the *Koran* to discover disgrace's torture,
never life in such as this be making it a forfeiture.

So, understand this, that ass is like your mind…

enslaved to it is worse than being, like her, blind!

That One gives to our forms the shape of an ass

for God makes forms like the inner, more or less!

Of Resurrection's secret this is a manifestation:

God's sake, for sake of God, flee a form asinine.

God terrified the unbelievers with the fear of fire,

and unbelievers said, "Better disgrace, than fire."

He replied, "No, the fire is the source of disgrace,"

like fire that killed this woman, in her own place.

From lustful greed she did not eat in moderation,

in her throat stuck a deadly inappropriate portion.

O you greedy man, partake in moderation only…

even if it is a mouthful of *halva* or *khabis*… only!

The Almighty, us a tongue for balance has given:

listen, recite chapter 'The Merciful' in the *Koran*.

Be careful not to let your balance be escaping you:

temptation and greed are enemies that entice you.

Greed desires everything, and loses everything…

Stinking son of a stinker, greed do not be serving!

That female servant left on her errand muttering,

"O mistress, this expert away you are sending...

you'll now try to do the thing without the expert,

and your life will be in danger without this expert.

O you, who stole from me imperfect knowledge...

too ashamed to ask of trick, the pumpkin wedge!"

If the bird hadn't picked the grain from the granary

trap's rope wouldn't have on neck fallen suddenly!

Do not eat so much grain, don't put on more fat...

after reciting 'Eat, drink,' recite 'No more of that,'

so you can eat the grain... yet not in the trap fall,

out of contentment and knowledge... that, is all!

One who is wise from the world takes happiness,

those who are ignorant take only... sorrowfulness.

When the trap's rope on their throats are falling,

it becomes unlawful for them, grain to be eating!

When can the bird in the trap be eating the grain?

The grain in the trap is like poison if eaten again!

Only the careless bird will from a trap grain eat,

like population of this world who such grain eat.

Again I say, the conscious birds aren't eating it:

they've made a wise decision not to be taking it,

because that grain in the trap is poisonous food
and that bird's blind that wants poisonous food.
Trap's Owner cuts off heads of the foolish ones
and to the assembly ushers the intelligent ones,
because in the former only the flesh is working...
and the wise ones soft and low are their singing.
That female servant through a crack in the door
her dead mistress lying under that ass she saw!
She called, "O foolish woman, what did you do?
Expert revealed little, trick was missed, by you!
Without becoming expert, the shop you opened:
his prick was just *halva* and honey you believed.
O lustful one, why you the pumpkin didn't see?
It was that you were by ass infatuated, maybe?
You saw only the outward work of this expert...
then happily you thought you were that expert."
Many a false master think they know the way
of the Sufis, wearers of wool, or... so they say.
O yes, there are a great many who are foolish
who've learnt from kings only to be a big fish!

All, with a staff in hand says, "I am Moses,"
then they breathe on fools saying, "I'm Jesus!"
Ah, no… for that Day when that touchstone
will be demanding of you to be sincere… alone.
Come here, and ask the Master for the rest…
or, are greedy ones blind, deaf, dumb at best?
You were craving all and you lost everything:
such a foolish flock as this wolves are eating!
From Master you heard and became teachers,
not knowing meaning of words… like parrots!

[The story of the jester Juhi who put on a chador and went to hear a sermon and a woman found out he was a man and screamed]

There was a preacher who was for his sermons respected,
under his pulpit many men and women were assembled.
Juhi put on his chador and veil and him he went to see...
he went among the women and none saw he was a 'he'.
Some one up the front then quietly asked the preacher...
"Does the pubic hair impede one when in ritual prayer?"
The preacher answered, "When one's pubic hair grows
too long... in the prayer an unwholesomeness follows.
One should use scissors or quicklime to them remove,
then upon your ritual prayer you can greatly improve."
The same questioner asked, "What must the length be
so that the ritual prayer near to perfect can then be?"
The reply was this, "O you devious rogue, if that hair
was to become like a grain of barley... cut that hair!"
Beside Juhi a woman was seated who was listening
intently to what that preacher had been instructing.

Juhi whispered to that woman, "Dear sister, quickly

look at whether my hair has grown as long as barley!

To please God, stretch out your hand and discover

if my pubic hair might with ritual prayer interfere!"

That woman obligingly placed her hand into his lap

under the clothing and at once his penis she did tap.

Immediately the woman screamed and the preacher

said... "My sermon, really reached the heart of her!

Ah, from this woman you can learn how to respond,

because my preaching has made her heart respond!"

Juhi answered, "No, it wasn't her heart responding

it was her hand that had been something touching!"

In case of the sorcerers of Pharaoh, when they were

struck, to them the hand and the staff as one were.

O reader, if you took stick from an old man he'd be

be more upset than loss of feet or hands by sorcery.

The shout of, "No harm!"* to Heaven reached up:

"Listen, cut them off for our souls the pain gave up.

"We now have knowledge that we're not the body:

we're living through God, we're beyond the body."

Blessed is one who has his real essence recognized
and a mansion in everlasting peace has fashioned.
The child for walnuts and for raisins is weeping...
but, for one who is mature they are a small thing.
In eye of soul like walnuts and raisins is the body:
how can a child attain what one mature can see?
That one who's veiled is a child in consciousness:
that one mature is beyond uncertainty... I stress!
If one claims to be a man due to a beard or balls...
then remember each male goat has a beard, balls!
Goat with beard and hairy balls is a bad leader...
that one, he is taking his followers to the butcher!
That one combed beard, saying, "I am, the one!"
You are the first... but only in death and in pain!
Listen, follow the light and the beard give away:
give away pride in self and worry, straight away,
so you become like the scent of the rose for lovers
of God so to rose-garden you lead all the lovers!
What is scent of the rose? It is breath of reason,
of intelligence, guide to the everlasting Garden.

(How Sultan Mahmud showed favour to his slave Ayaz)

"O Ayaz, in your ways you are humble, full of sincerity
and greater than the sea and mountains is your honesty.
There is no stumbling for you in the moment of lust, so
your mind is like a mountain, like straw it doesn't blow.
In the hour of rage and anger, your powers of endurance
and steadfastness never fail to be making their stance."
Such traits are true manliness, not a beard or a penis...
if it was not the case that of an ass is the bigger penis!
In the *Koran* who's it that God has described as 'men'?
As He stated can there be any room for the body, then?
O my son, what then is the worth of any animal's soul?
Come though the bazaar of butchers and see the whole
heads of hundreds of thousands of animals laid out on
worth less than the fat near the tail or tail hanging on.
Try not to be a servant of lust or it will be your home:
don't mortgage heart, it will throw you in a dungeon!
A good whore would be one whose mind becomes like
a mouse and lust like a lion seeing a penis' first strike.

SADI

Musharrif-ud-din bin Muslih-ud-din 'Abdu'llah, is better known under his poetical pen-name or *takhallus* of 'Sadi' (meaning 'fortunate'), which was acquired either from his first patron, the ruler of Fars, Atabeg Sa'd b. Zangi, whose ascension to the throne took place in 1195 and who died in 1226... or his son, also named Sa'd: Abu Bakr ibn Sa'd ibn Zangi (ruled 1226-60) to whom Sadi dedicated his *Bustan* or *Orchard* in 1257 and his most famous work the *Gulistan* or *Rose Garden* a year later. Sadi was born at Fars' capital... the beautiful, fabled city of Shiraz, in south-west Persia, around 1208.

Terror, plunder, rape and murder on a vast scale engulfed Persia during the thirteenth century at the hands of the Mongols... but, fortunately Shiraz, in the mountains of the south-west, was almost unaffected. It was a cultured and famously beautiful city with wise and enlightened rulers that passed on to future generations its great traditions of culture and civilized life from past ages.

'The Mongols, surpassing in cruelty the most barbarous people, murdered in cold blood, in the conquered countries, men, women and children; burned towns and villages; transformed flourishing lands into deserts; and yet were animated by neither hate nor vengeance, for indeed they hardly knew the names of the peoples whom they exterminated. One would suppose that history had exaggerated their atrocities, were not the annals of all countries in agreement on this point. After the conquest, one sees the Mongols treat as slaves under a frightful tyranny those whom the sword had spared. Their government was the triumph of depravity; all that was noble and honorable was abased, while the most corrupt men, attaching themselves to the service of these ferocious masters, obtained, as the price of their vile devotion, riches, honors, and the power to oppress their fellow-countrymen. The history of the Mongols, therefore, stamped with their barbarity, offers only hideous pictures, though, being closely connected with that of several empires, it is necessary for a proper understanding of the great events of the thirteenth and fourteenth centuries.' Baron d'Ohsson. *Histoire des Mongols. Paris 1834-5.*

Sadi's father, 'Abdu'llah, was a descendant of Ali, the cousin and son-in-law of the Prophet, and was for some time in difficult circumstances, but having obtained a petty government appointment through an influential patron, his zeal, ability and integrity raised him in the estimation of his superiors and gained for him a promotion and opened up a prospect of future advancement. Unfortunately, he died while Sadi was a child of ten or eleven, leaving him and his mother a small amount of money which soon disappeared through the intrigues of false friends and Sadi and his mother were obliged to live for a time either on the bounty of the Atabeg, or some say a relative who was probably his uncle on his mother's side, the celebrated Mulla Kutb, the learned disciple of Khwaja Nasiruddin of Tus. This story is remarkably similar to that of Shiraz's next great poet and master of the poetic form of the *ghazal*, Hafiz, who also lost his father at a similar age and he and his mother were forced to live with his uncle... named *Sadi!* Nizami, the other great Persian Master of the *ghazal* form of poetry was also orphaned and went to live with an uncle! In this poem from his *Bustan* Sadi laments the fate of not having a father...

You should protect the orphan... whose father is dead,

brush mud from his clothes, stop pain hitting his head.

You don't know how hard for him living happens to be:

when the root is cut away... does life exist in the tree?

Do not hug and do not kiss that child that is your own

where an orphan can see it... so neglected and so alone!

If the orphan cries tears, who will comfort his suffering?

If he loses his temper... who his rage will be believing?

You make sure he doesn't cry, for surely God's throne

begins to shake violently from the orphan's sad moan.

With pity that is infinite... and with most tender care,

wipe tears from his eyes... and brush dust from his hair.

There's not a shield of parental protection over his head

sheltering him: you, be that protector he needs, instead.

When the arms of a father around my neck could fold...

way back then I was crowned like a monarch, with gold.

Back then, if even a fly should come and alight upon me:

not one heart... many, were scared by what they'd see!

But now, if I'm taken captive and they do what they will,

I call out loud, but no friend comes, no matter how shrill!

Sorrows of orphans I can always understand... and share,

way back in my childhood... I tasted the orphan's despair.

Sadi mentions his mother in his *Gulistan* (chapter 6,

story 6)… 'One day, due to the ignorance and folly of youth, I shouted at my mother. She was cut to the heart and she sat in a corner and began to cry, saying: "Perhaps you've forgotten being the time you were an infant, that you would speak to me so harshly." '

Sadi completed his early years of education in Shiraz and during this time Sa'd b. Zangi (the First) fought a drawn-out eight-year war with his cousin to keep the throne but this long struggle had devastating consequences. The young Sadi was passionately fond of learning, and, in pursuit of knowledge, determined to travel to Baghdad at that time famed for its learned men and schools. He states in his preface to his Gulistan…

> *Do you know why, as an outcast and exile…*
>
> *in lands of a stranger I sought refuge for awhile?*
>
> *World was unraveling like an Ethiopian's hair,*
>
> *when I fled the Turks and their reign… terror!*

On arrival at Baghdad his prospects were not so good, as he was without money and was a stranger. He was fortunate in relating his tale to a wealthy and benevolent inhabitant of the city, who sympathized with him, and provided for to go to a private school. He worked hard and when he twenty-one years of age composed some verses of poetry that he dedicated to a professor of literature in the famous Nizameh College. The professor was so pleased with the poem that he gave Sadi an allowance and promised to assist him in his literary pursuits. Soon Sadi gained admission to the Nizameh College and by his intelligence and effort, aided by able instructors, obtained a scholarship that enabled him to pursue his studies comfortably.

There his teachers included the great Sufi Master and teacher Shaikh Abdul Kader Gilani from whom he leaned the nature of Divinity and Sufi doctrine. It is said that he also met the Sufi Perfect Master (Qutub) Shihab al-Din al-Suhrawardi (d.1234) the founder of a famous order of dervishes. Under the Caliph, Mutasim-Billah, the youngest son of the much celebrated Harun-ar-Rashid, the court of Baghdad had become corrupt and the government weak. The Mongol chief, Hulagu Khan had overrun the province and hearing of the state of anarchy existing in Baghdad he besieged the city and eventually he captured it. His soldiers sacked the city and pillaged and murdered and raped. The Caliph and his family was cruelly put to death. Sadi laments this in a *qasida...*

It is proper for tears of blood from the heavens upon the earth to flow,

for ruler of the Faithful, Caliph al-Mutasim has been felled, so low!

If, Mohammed, at the Judgment from the dust your head you raise...

raise it now and witness the Judgment fallen upon your people below!

Great waves of blood overwhelm the low thresholds of the palace beauties...

as out from my heart blood of my life dyes these sleeves, colour of woe!

Be afraid how Fortune changes quickly and the fast turning of the Sphere...

who could ever even dream that such splendour such a fate could overthrow?

Raise your eyes, O all of you who once upon that Holy House did look,

watching Khans and Caesars that cringing, under its portals did go.

Now, on that same threshold where many kings their foreheads laid, from children of the Uncle of the Prophet streams of blood now flow!

Sadi fled with his Master Shaikh Gilani... to Mecca, the first of fifteen pilgrimages he would make to that place.

After leaving the college at the age of twenty-seven he then spent thirty years wandering and traveling as a poor dervish throughout many lands and had many adventures and the people he met and the spiritual and worldly knowledge he acquired on these extensive travels (he has been called 'The Marco Polo of the East') he recorded when he finally came home to Shiraz in 1256. He wrote them down in his *Bustan* and *Gulistan* in moral and even ribald stories and sayings and philosophy in poetry *(Bustan)* and in poetry and prose *(Gulistan)* that would bring him both fame and fortune at home and in many lands. Both would be dedicated to the son of Atabeg Sa'd b. Zangi, Abu Bakr ibn Sa'd ibn Zangi... who took over ruler-ship of Shiraz after his father died in 1226.

'The *Bustan,* which like all poems of proverbial wisdom defies adequate translation, had brought its author immediate fame which the passing centuries have only served to increase. In later years calligraphers and artists delighted to copy and illustrate it for wealthy patrons of art and letters, who have never been wanting in Persia, and so produced some of the great manuscripts of the world. The *Gulistan* scored an equal success, and emperors have been proud to see it adorn their libraries. Not only so, but both books, being written in simple yet correct and most elegant Persian, have served many generations as models of how to write, and both books, being replete with the kind of pithy sentiments schoolmasters love to inculcate, have been compulsory reading in every seminary of Persia for nearly seven hundred years. It would be no exaggeration to say that they, after the *Koran*, have done most to shape the Persian outlook.' A.J. Arberry.

From Sadi's *Bustan* or 'Orchard'. He gives the reason why he composed the book...

I traveled much throughout the world's distant places,
and I've passed much time with those of different races.
From each corner where I ventured I discovered pleasure,
and I did obtain from many a harvest, many a corn's ear.
Like those pure folk of Shiraz who are as humble as dust
I have never seen another: mercy be on that place's dust.
Cultivating of friendship of the men of this sacred land,

from Syria and Turkey turned away my heart and hand.

From all of those fragrant gardens of the world I wanted

to bring to my friends something, not be empty-handed.

I said to myself... "From Egypt, one often brings sugar,

it's done so, brought home to friends, a present to offer!"

And, even though these hands of mine carry no sugar...

in my possession I've words that than sugar are sweeter:

and not that kind of sugar that men may happen to eat;

but, the kind that is kept on paper, a more lasting treat!

When this palace of great wealth I had finally designed

I did build into it ten doors of instructions for the mind.

The first is a chapter on Justice and Good Judgment...

how to care for the people and to fear God's Judgment.

The second chapter: I laid the foundation of Generosity;

for one in being generous, is praising God's Generosity.

The third is about Love and Madness and Intoxication;

but, not that worldly love, that men usually dwell upon.

Sadi goes on to list the other seven doors or chapters...
Humility, Resignation, Contentment, Education,
Gratitude, Repentance, Prayer.

Emerson, appreciating the *Gulistan* on reading
Gladwin's translation, wrote this at Concord in 1864. 'Sadi,

though he has not the lyric flights of Hafiz, has wit, practical sense, and just moral sentiments. He has the instinct to teach, and from every occurrence must draw the moral, like Franklin. He is the poet of friendship, love, self-devotion, and serenity. There is a uniform force in his page, and conspicuously, a tone of cheerfulness, which has almost made his name a synonym for this grace. The word *Sadi* means *fortunate*. In him the trait is no result of levity, much less of convivial habit, but first of a happy nature, to which victory is habitual, easily shedding mishaps, with sensibility to pleasure, and with resources against pain. But it also results from the habitual perception of the beneficent laws that control the world. He inspires in the reader a good hope. What a contrast between the cynical tone of Byron and the benevolent wisdom of Sadi! By turns, a student, a water-carrier, a traveler, a soldier fighting against the Christians in the Crusades, a prisoner employed to dig trenches before Tripoli, and an honored poet in his protracted old age at home: his varied and severe experience took away all provincial tone and gave him a facility of speaking to all conditions. But the commanding reason of his wider popularity is his deeper sense, which, in his treatment, expands the local forms and tints to a cosmopolitan breadth. Through his Persian dialect he speaks to all nations, and, like Homer, Shakespeare, Cervantes, and Montaigne, is perpetually modern.'

His thirty years of travels on foot and every other way took him through many countries in Mesopotamia, Asia Minor, North Africa, Arabia and to Syria and probably into India (though recent studies dispute that he went there). He said, 'I have wandered to various regions of the world and everywhere I've mixed freely with the inhabitants, gathering something in each corner, gleaning an ear from every harvest.'

Some of his travels brought him into very difficult circumstances. On one occasion in the Holy Land he was taken prisoner by the Franks and was finally ransomed but had to pay the ransom back by marrying a wife who made his life a misery, as he states in the *Gulistan*...

'Weary of the society of my friends at Damascus I fled to the barren wastes of Jerusalem, and associated with brutes, until I was made captive by the Franks, and forced to dig clay, along with Jews, in the fortifications of Tripoli. One of the nobles of Aleppo, an old friend, happened to pass that way and remembered me, saying, "What a state you're in... how are you?" I answered, "Seeing that I could place confidence in God alone. I retired to the mountains and wilds to avoid the society of man; but judge what is now my situation, that I am confined in a trench in company with wretches who deserve not the name of men. To be chained by the feet, with friends, is better than to be free to walk in a garden with strangers." He took compassion on my forlorn condition, ransomed me from the Franks for ten *dinars* and took me with him to Aleppo. My friend had a daughter, to whom he married me, and presented me with one hundred *dinars* as her dowry. After some time my wife unveiled her disposition, which was bad-tempered, quarrelsome, obstinate and abusive, so that the happiness of my life vanished. It has been well said, "A bad woman, in the house of a virtuous man is his hell, even in this world. Take care not to connect yourself with a bad woman. Save us, O Lord, from this fiery trial!" Once she reproached me with the following taunt: "Aren't you the creature whom my father ransomed from captivity amongst the Franks for ten *dinars?*" "Yes," I answered, "he redeemed me for ten *dinars* and enslaved me to you for a hundred." I heard that a great man once rescued a sheep from the mouth of a wolf, but at night drew his knife across his throat. The expiring sheep thus complained, "You delivered me certainly from the jaws of a wolf, but in the end, I perceive that you have yourself become a wolf to me." '

Sadi had more luck in his second marriage and was said to have had a son and a daughter. The son whom he loved very much died in childhood and his untimely end was a source of great grief to him.

Sadi's amazing travels and stories, morality and philosophy and poetry can be discovered though his two books the *Gulistan* and the *Bustan* and as stated these two works have been a great influence on the whole world ever since.

On returning to Shiraz he penned his two most-famous works and with the vast proceeds built a hostel near the 'God is Great' Gate to Shiraz where travelers could stay, get refreshments and wash their clothes. This location later became that of his tomb.

Two years after Sadi finished his *Gulistan* and dedicated it to his patron Abu Bakr ibn Sa'd as he did a year earlier with his *Bustan,* on May 18, 1260 Shiraz's ruler died and his son who had waited long for his chance at ruler-ship died within two weeks. His baby son Muhammad succeeded him, but his life ended in two years in 1262.

Sadi is credited with having worked some miracles, especially that of restoring to life a young lover, who had cast himself down from a tower, one hundred feet high, to the ground.

According to 'Shaikh' Sadi, he was modest in manner and could not tolerate vanity in others. He dressed modestly, was short in stature, thin and like Hafiz was not handsome and was soon bald; but a face beaming with intelligence and a long-flowing beard that gave him an engaging and venerable appearance.

His written works consists not only of his two most famous books (in the West) the *Bustan* and the *Gulistan*. In fact his *Kulliyat* or 'Collected Works' consists of twenty-four separate volumes including a volume of *Khabissat* or 'Indecencies' that he claimed in the Introduction he was forced to compose by 'one of the descendants of the king' who threatened him with death if he did not do so! He then asks God to forgive him... but adds that such stories and poetry are like 'salt in food'.

His *Khabissat* that appears only in some editions of his collected works but is considered genuine consists of three parts... Poems, Assemblies of Jests and Pleasantries, Jokes in prose.

Selected Bibliography

Divan of Sadi: His Mystical Love Poems, Translation by Paul Smith, New Humanity Books, Campbells Creek, 2012.

Suppressed Persian. An Anthology of Forbidden Literature. Translated with Notes and an Introduction by Paul Sprachman. Mazda Publications. 1995. (See pages 33-44).

Tayyibat. The Odes of Sheikh Muslihu'd-Din Sa'di Shirazi. Translated by Sir Lucas White King. Luzac & Co. London, 1926.

Badayi. The Odes of Sheikh Muslihu'd-Din Sa'di Shirazi. Translated by Sir Lucas White King. Kaviani Press 1925.

Ruba'iyat of Sadi, Translation and Introduction by Paul Smith. New Humanity Books, Campbells Creek, 2012.

Sadi: Selected Poems, Translation & Introduction by Paul Smith, New Humanity Books, Campbells Creek 2012.

The Bustan by Shaikh Muslihu-D-Din Sa'di Shirazi. Translated by H. Wilberforce Clarke, R.E. 1879. Darf Publishers Limited. 1985.

The Garden of Fragrance: Being A Complete Translation of The Bostan of Sadi... From the Original Persian into English Verse By G.S. Davie, M.D. Keegan, Paul, Trench and Co. London. 1882.

Morals Pointed & Tales Adorned, The Bustan of Sadi, Trans. by G. M. Wickens. University of Toronto Press. 1974.

The Gulistan or Rose Garden of Sa'di. Translated by Edward Rehatsek. Kama Sutra Society. 1888. New Humanity Books 1988.

The Poet Sa'di: A Persian Humanist By John D. Yohannan. Rowman & Littlefield Publishers Inc. 1987. (A mine of information of the life, poetry and influence on the west of Sadi and a chapter on his 'indecencies'))

Hafiz of Shiraz: by Paul Smith, New Humanity Books, Campbells Creek. 2000-9. (Throughout this long 'living biography' written from the oldest Persian and other sources using Creative Imagination or himma' the verse and influence of Sadi on later poets and the Shirazis is evident).

Shiraz in the Age of Hafez. The Glory of a Medieval City. John Limbert. University of Washington Press. 2004. (See in particular chapters 1 & 2.)

RUBA'IS...

Some idiot's wife from him got a divorce...
found another husband as a matter of course.
One had hands on head from wife's betrayal
the others prick was left to its own resource.

Due to you drunken eye, I see a hope of

sleeping...

you slept well while I did not, as I was

worrying.

I cannot be truly satisfied only with you

watching...

my tale's such that it I cannot really be

telling.

If some hermaphrodite by a Tartar was killed,

in retribution the Tartar should not be killed:

how long will one be like a Baghdad's bridge,

on top a man, underneath that coming liquid?

If you are a good man of the people of religion...
then you should only be choosing masturbation.
What can be beaten than at the time of fucking
you can see the head after the prick is placed in?

MASNAVI...

Once, heart and mind of a learned Sufi were enchained
by the face and curls of a boy, who was well-endowed.
He was a strong wrestler, with many a hard muscle...
with a gazelle's eyes so flirtatious, but arms like steel!
Day after day he did nothing but try to think of a way
that he could one night make that boy come his way...
he hotly went after that one, hoping to grab his apple,
that musky-smelling fruit he wanted to kiss... if able!
Inside the loin-cloth of that wrestler he wanted to go,
and fire up his dart up it's crack as far as he could go.
But that catamite was rough and his temper was hot,
he threatened with the whip and fist... all he had got!
He shouted at him, "I'll never let you be shaming me,
I'll not let you face down on the floor be pinning me...
but should my embraces and kisses be enough for you
I'm the youth for you... come with me you can! You?"
That Sufi answered him, "With me this will be fine...
O cypress-tree formed one, O my young man so fine,

all I wish to do is take you into these arms, embrace

you and drop dead before your beauty, in any place."

The fears of the wrestler were laid to rest, by this…

he went up to that Sufi and on cheek planted a kiss.

They then embrace like two almonds in one shell…

lip against lip they melded in a lust, like from hell!

As soft throat of that boy that Sufi was caressing,

his lust was so great his penis was almost busting.

Then, without any warning he lost all control of it,

it slipped along his side and into his hole it did fit.

All patience disappeared, lust was the conqueror,

the standard of the Sufi was planted, even deeper.

That youth cried, "Ah no… have you gone crazy?

Why treat me like an animal, why such cruelty?"

But, his heart was gone, what could the Sufi do…

when true love arrives, about it what can one do?

Into the hand of that youth he some coins placed,

because even muscles the gold has never resisted.

Then that tempting boy his house for sale put up:

he said, "Drive in your arrow… push it right up!"

That God-seeker, now was no longer suffering,
he went into the house, again it he was entering.
To friends and companions he brought that boy,
and he passed him one to the other for their joy.
Each one received a kiss from the youth or two,
they studied his naval, probing his rectum, too.
One of them told him he was in love, devoted...
another told to him he was by him worshipped.
Among them scandal, turmoil was spreading...
the uproar was so loud the sky it was reaching.
Their necks became black and blue from blows,
the Order from stones, hits, was 'on the nose'.
The master of all those *kalandars** they visited
and him what was occurring... they informed.
With his head lowered he was deeply thinking
and eventually he raised it and he was saying:
"We all share our food, as our Oder is so poor:
for ten, one pair of shoes is enough... or more!"
Of what he said all of them were approving...
they had his word their wounds to be healing.

They prostrated before him... him they praised

in poems and in songs that they then chanted!

That wrestler, who had never been defeated...

had his brow now to the mat pinned, defeated!

And so he repented and wanted to give up men

all those who were saddened had to wait, then.

Note: True kalandars are lovers of God who have given up attachment to desires and live only for God. The name comes from a Master named Kalandar Yusuf. The word means 'pure gold.'

PROSE

O Muslims, I have a penis that isn't a Sufi but its head is bald, and it's no ascetic but into a cave it goes and it's not blind but it has just one eye.

A man was sitting and his prick could be seen and his son saw it and said, "Daddy, that... is what?" His father replied, "It is your daddy's foot!" The son asked, "Where then is the shoe for the foot?" His father answered, "Your mummy has an old slipper that occasionally daddy puts on his foot!"

Someone said, "Tonight the one performing a special prayer will receive a huri whose form stretches from the eastern horizon to the western horizon." Another answered, "I'm not saying it, I don't want her." Others asked him, "Why?" "He replied, If her head was beside me and they were fucking her in Baghdad and Shiraz, would I know it?"

OBEYD ZAKANI

Obeyd Zakani (Nizam ud-Din Obeydu'llah) was born in 1300 in the small village of Zakan ten miles north-west of the city of Qazvin in the north of Persia (about a hundred miles west from Tehran). His family was one of the notable tribes of the area, Sunnite members of the Islamic aristocracy, descended from the Arabian tribe of Khafaja.

Mirza Habib states in his preface to Obeyd's works published in 1885... "That most witty poet Obeyd Zakani was of the village of Zakan near Qazvin, and was one of the notabilities of the eighth century of the Flight (14th century A.D.). He was a man of talent and learning, one of the masters of style and sound taste. Although some reckon him as one of the ribald writers, it is only fair to state that although jests, ribaldry and satire occur in his poems... he deserves to rank as something more than a mere satirist, being indeed conspicuous amongst the older poets for his grace and wit, and in these respects approached by few. He was particularly skilful in incorporating in his poems and investing with a ludicrous sense the serious verses of other poets, an achievement in which he left no ground unturned.

His own serious poems on the other hand, are incomparable in fluency of diction, sweetness and distinction, and are unrivalled in grace and subtlety.

"Obeyd Zakani pursued his studies at Shiraz... At that time the Turks in Persia had left no prohibited or vicious act undone, and the character of the Persian people, by reason of association and intercourse with them, had become so changed and corrupted that Obeyd Zakani, disgusted at the contemplation thereof, sought by every means to make known and bring home to them the true condition of affairs. Therefore, as an example of the corrupt morals of the age and its people, he composed the treatise known as the *Ethics of the Nobles* that was not intended as mere ribaldry but as a satire containing serious reflections and wise warnings. So likewise, in order to depict the level of intelligence and degree of knowledge of the leading men of Qazwin, each one of whom was a mass of stupidity and ignorance, he included in his *Joyous Treatise* many anecdotes of which each contains a lesson for persons of discernment. As a measure of his accomplishments, experience, learning and worldly wisdom, his *A Hundred Maxims* and his *Definitions* are a sufficient proof."

The early 1330's found Obeyd in Baghdad at the Court of the young sultan Abu Said. The Court poet at the time was an older poet Khaju Kermani (1291-1352) whom it is said Obeyd took an instant dislike to and the feeling was returned. Later Khaju would take up the position of Court poet in Shiraz and annoy Obeyd even more. As the situation at Court was now so difficult, Obeyd made his way to Shiraz in the south (where Masud Shah, the eldest son of Mahmud Shah whom the successor to Sultan Abu Said had recently put to death, now ruled)... in search of a teaching position and perhaps a royal patron. He would spend the next eighteen years there, the most productive period of his life in many ways.

Shiraz in the 14th century, famous for its gardens, wine, poets and beautiful women, almost miraculously was spared the atrocities and genocide that the Mongols had committed in most of Persia in the previous century. The depth of depravity and cruelty of the Mongols towards the Persians has probably not been equaled in all of known history.

As for the previous seven hundred years Shiraz had been ruled over by non-Shirazis and in the past two hundred by those of Turkish or Mongol origin the population had accepted the idea that they were born to rule over them and the ruler of Shiraz's father, Mahmud Shah, though not Turkish himself, had a Turkish wife Tashi Khatun (the mother of his youngest son, Abu Ishak, who was greatly loved and influential in her own right. She endowed many public buildings including a college... and often paid her respects at the tomb of the Spiritual Master Ibn Khafif known as Shaikh-e-Kabir who was credited with having brought Sufism to Shiraz four hundred years earlier.

Junaid Shirazi a poet and historian of Shiraz at the time, wrote in his book on Shiraz about the shrines of the many Saints and Spiritual Masters who had graced this place with their presence and where Shirazis weekly or even daily went on pilgrimage. This was usually a surprisingly joyous and relaxed occasion with a picnic-like atmosphere and a chance to socialize with family and friends. There are many important pilgrimage shrines apart from that of Shaikh-e-Kabir that is in the northern Darb-e-Istakhr quarter.

An understanding of the multi-layered and interlocking and often conflicting structure of Shirazi society is essential to the understanding the satire and social commentary and poetry and ribaldry of Obeyd at that time. On top was the ruler and although he was in power he usually did not directly control the everyday goings-on of the city. All of that was designated to officials such as the minister for police, tax-collectors, bazaar regulators, who were appointed by the prime minister. The prime-minister's life was often shortened if he antagonized in some way his master or if the king was deposed.

Those that were most powerful and influential amongst the nobles were the fourteen hundred *sayyids* (or descendants of the Prophet) who received from the government yearly stipends. The Shirazi *sayyids* controlled much wealth in the city and did so by endowments of colleges and individuals and events. Such wealth and power also meant they were somewhat independent from the ruler and their ruler, their *naqib,* like the chief-judge wielded much power upwards and downwards.

Apart from the ruler, chief-judge and *naqib,* the various trade guilds leaders and neighbourhood groups were of much importance in how the city functioned. The king had to have the support of such organization's leaders or bosses who had the responsibility to keep order in the bazaars and seventeen quarters and if the city was under siege they oversaw the battlements and security of all the gates. These bosses tried to control the street ruffians, young so-called 'heroes' and gangs that were potential mobs that could be for or against the rulers.

Under these chiefs were the common workers who could easily join the mobs in the street if the occasion arose and the ruler was hated. Some were ridiculed by the nobles and called drunken rogues and reprobate-outsiders (rindan), ruffians and no-hopers but such young men saw themselves as heroes (pahlavan), and believed in the lore of chivalry and their groups welcomed and fed and housed strangers and gave protection to the weak and vulnerable when violent times befell the city. Obeyd was often identifying himself with the rindan but his rindan belief was more about an inner philosophy of rejection of the outer forms of hypocritical society and religious dogma and rituals and a freedom to reject reason in favour of love and divine-intoxication, although he often expressed his rejection through poems and satire and obscene stories and sayings.

Apart from the chief-judges, leaders of the sayyids and the bosses of the guilds and neighbourhoods there was another group who wielded great power... even though they were not appointed by the ruler. These were the shaikhs and their families. The shaikhs were the head-preachers and Sufi leaders, such as the evil and powerful black-magician Shaikh Ali Kolah who claimed he could control the *jinn*... and the false *zahid* or ascetic Abdullah bin Jiri were deep and dangerous thorns in Obeyd's side for all the years he was there. He states in this *ruba'i*...

Don't believe anything that shaikh says to you

then you won't go to Hell... won't get lost too!

Avoid talking to that zahid, the false ascetic...

so leaving a place with a smile on face you do.

On arriving in 1335 Obeyd fell in love with the city and joyfully proclaimed in a *ghazal*...

Perfume from Musalla's garden and Ruknabad's pure water

drive off thoughts of home from mind of an exiled traveller.

O resting place most blessed, realm that enlivens this life;

may your foundations beyond compare, continue to prosper!

Every corner that one settles in, the nightingale is singing;

if meadow's visited, box-tree growing in loveliness is there.

No matter where you look a beauty like Shirin does shine,

wherever you walk further a lover like Farhad sighs for her.

Understand as valuable fortune when good luck offers joy,

for the human form's weak and life's foundation is weaker.

Hold tight skirt of one you love and do whatever you want:

drink pure bright wine and let be what happens: whatever!

Turn towards the wine and cry of flute... because it is said

that man comes from air and the world is set upon water.

The delicate charms of this world are truly sweet, but like

Obeyd, I'm the slave of that man who in it is not a believer.

By 1338 Obeyd had found a position teaching at one of the smaller colleges in Shiraz and at that time there was (most likely) one of his pupils... who was then eighteen years old, small and ugly, and working in a drapery shop and studying at night. His father who was a coal-merchant from Isfahan had died when he was seven and he and his mother who was from Kazerun were left destitute and were forced to go and live with his uncle, Sadi... who considered himself a poet like his famous namesake, Sadi of Shiraz, who had died about fifty years earlier and was still the most popular poet in the city. He and another Master Poet, Nizami, had greatly influenced the young man with such a remarkable memory that by the age of eight he had memorized the whole of the *Koran...* and Sadi's poems, and hence Shams-ud-din Mohammad took 'Hafiz' as his poetic pen-name or *takhallus* (one who knows the *Koran* by heart).

He was determined to emulate his hero and had gained some notoriety with his poems in praise of the new king that he had read to mild applause in the various tea-houses he frequented. These poems had come to the attention of the king's prime-minister, the wealthy and much-loved patron of the arts, Khwaja Haji Kivam... and so Hafiz received an invitation to read them at the gathering of poets *(musha'irah)* during the king's New Year's garden party... an event that Masud Shah had decided to revive, being a lover of wine, music and poetry as was his father.

Also invited, along with many of Shiraz's esteemed poets was one of his teachers, Obeyd Zakani, who on arrival in Shiraz had found little interest in his serious writings and being a natural comic and satirist decided that the role of court-jester might be the way to get a finger into the royal purse-strings. He states in this *ruba'i*...

In arts and learning don't be clever like me:
or like me, by the 'great', hated you will be.
You want plaudits from such a time as this?
Musician, drunkard, or shameless beggar be!
And in another...
Sir, stay clear of knowledge, if it happens you stay,
or you will lose the pittance that you will get today;
play the fool and learn well the skills of... the fiddle,
upon great and small you can then... will-fully, play!

At this poetry gathering came together for probably the first time Iran's greatest mystical, lyric poet, Hafiz; its greatest satirist and social commentator, Obeyd Zakani, and its greatest female poet Princess Jahan Malek.

Jahan's father, Shiraz's ruler Masud Shah, proudly introduced into the gathering of Shiraz's most important poets his sixteen year old daughter who was petite and extraordinarily beautiful and already somewhat too liberated for the upper-class nobility that were shocked that this mere slip of a girl had the audacity to consider herself as a poet... a problem that she would encounter for the rest of her life as she states in her Preface to her large collection of poems, "I composed poems all day long. Sometimes untalented and lazy people teased or found fault with me. Only some people are able to compose poetry. If composing poems is so bad we wouldn't have so many poets. At first I thought it wasn't a good occupation because it was disapproved of and not liked in the society that I lived in. After sometime I realized that our Prophet Mohammed's daughter composed poems and other women too, including his wife Ayesha. I began to compose poems everyday... it became my pleasure."

Obeyd, who already had a reputation as having a roving eye for beautiful members of either sex (the younger the better) was immediately under her spell and began composing poems about her...

One more time... my head I'm losing:

with my heart, once more I'm playing.

She, is a princess... and I'm ordinary:

she, is a queen... and now I'm begging!

Lithe figure and long braid like a lasso:

queen of beauty, my heart she's ruling.

Her eyebrows are wide like a bent bow:

waist slim: dark, magical: she's lying!

A charming flirt, graceful and straight

like cypress: a juggler, she's cheating.

Without her, I have no light from sun:

no her... no purity in world I'm seeing.

Place where her ruby lips start to smile

sugar loses all of its value, I'm saying!

In my heart always, never from mind:

when with her... lovingly I'm talking.

Going to her is like going to a doctor:

relief for my aching heart I'm hoping.

Everyone complains about an enemy:

only of this friend... I'm complaining!

If Obeyd's eyes get a real look at her...

her from all calamities I'm protecting!

Princess Jahan was already quite proficient in composing the simple four-lined *ruba'i*, but it was the more complicated *ghazal* that fascinated her and which led her to ask her father to find her a teacher of this form that at the time was being sung at Court and in the markets and winehouses, the most popular compositions being those of Shiraz's Sadi and the great Nizami.

The *ghazal* is a unique form and its origin has been argued about for many centuries. Some say that the *ghazal* originated in songs that were composed in Persia to be sung at court before Persia was converted to Islam, but not one song has survived to prove this. It is also possible that originally the *ghazals* were songs of love that were sung by minstrels in the early days of Persian history and that this form passed into poetry down the ages. This explanation is plausible for the following reasons: firstly, the word *ghazal* means 'a conversation between lovers.' Secondly, the *ghazals* of Obeyd, Hafiz, Sadi, Jahan and others were often put to music and became songs, which have been popular in Persia from ancient times until now.

In his important work on Obeyd, Hasan Javadi states in his *The Ethics of the Aristocrats and Other Satirical Works...* Jahan Books Co. 1985 page 18: "... he is a great and remarkable poet, especially in his *ghazals*, which are both charming and beautiful and present an interesting contrast to his satirical works."

Obeyd would most likely have offered his services in regard to teaching Jahan this poetic form but it was the small and ugly young Hafiz that attracted her for this position, even though his *ghazals* at that time could not be compared to those of the much older poet and were in fact quite pedestrian copies of his hero, the great Sadi. With Hafiz there would be no romantic complications, both she and her father understood. He was hired on a small stipend with Masud Shah asking his chief adviser Khwaja Haji Kivam who had already seen a poet of promise and a remarkable 'memorizer' in the young Hafiz, to look after the details.

It would be two years before an event would occur that would make Hafiz and his eventually remarkable *ghazals* the talk of the city and lead to a friendship between the two young poets that would last all their lifetimes. But her relationship with Obeyd would be a strange and stormy one, often swerving between contempt and fascination and lust and jealousy. This *ruba'i* of Jahan's was probably about the later short time physical aspect of their relationship...

My loved one, calming my heart down is:

they all tell me that he... an ugly clown is.

He may not seem to be beautiful to others,

but to me he is and beside me lying down is.

Her father the king, Masud Shah, having recently experienced the treachery of his brother Kaikhosrau (who had slyly taken the crown from him but was eventually disposed of) was ripe for even false rumours at his Court about possible seditious actions of his second youngest brother the hapless, but faithful Mohammad. He let his paranoia get the better of him and without telling Tashi Khatun, his father's wife who was the mother of his youngest brother Abu Ishak, and who was greatly revered by all the brothers and especially Jahan and all of the people of Shiraz as a loving, intelligent and saintly soul... he had his brother arrested in the dead of night and sent to prison in the castle-fortress at Safid. When news spread throughout

Shiraz that this had happened his popularity took a sudden plunge but... after all, he was their king and perhaps his brother was up to something?

Fearing the growing power and ambitions of the fierce fighter and ruler of Yazd, Mubariz Muzaffar (who would later feature as the 'cat' in Obeyd's epic *qasida 'Mouse and Cat'*, he sent his youngest brother the handsome and brave and poetry-writing Abu Ishak to take some of the army to Yazd to 'persuade' Mubariz to agree to annex his holdings to that of the province of Fars and accept governorship under him, Masud Shah.

After much bloody fighting and negotiations Mubariz signed an agreement to accept this, but as Abu Ishak informed his brother on return he was a most untrustworthy soul and a tough opponent of incredible strength and bravery.

After a little over a year of imprisonment in the fortress of Safid Masud Shah's brother, Mohammad, escaped and made his way to the camp of Pir Husain the Chupanid, known by all not only to be ambitious but quite ruthless. Possibly Pir Husain sent someone in there to free him, then he could march on Shiraz with a 'legitimate' heir to the throne and there were still many in Shiraz who felt

Mohammad was terribly wronged by his brother. For two weeks in 1339 Masud Shah and the people of the city stood up to Pir Husain and his army even though his troops outnumbered them. After losing half his soldiers Masud Shah sent a message to Pir Husain and his brother Mohammad that at noon, in two hours, the gates would open and they could march into the city to the palace and that he would be gone. He escaped with a few guards and advisers down a tunnel that lead from the palace to one of the larger underground *qanats* that took them well beyond the outskirts of the city and to safety. Masud Shah's mother and his daughter Princess Jahan decided to stay and hide out among the people. Masud Shah fled to Lauristan to find someone powerful to help him to try to take back Shiraz. Within a month the hapless brother Mohammad was executed by Pir Husain and then he had the youngest brother Abu Ishak and his mother the much loved, courageous and beautiful Tashi Khatun dragged through the city to be then taken to Tabriz to be questioned about her husband's wealth and property. The people rose up, this being the final insult (after the senseless death of

Mohammad) and freed them after she pleaded to the population in the name of her much-loved husband.

Most likely Hafiz and Obeyd Zakani were involved in this revolution that eventually led to the populace attacking the palace and Pir Husain fleeing the city after losing many of his soldiers and much of his claimed booty. The Shirazis were a fighting and gallant people as will be often seen!

During 1340 amongst all this confusion Obeyd finally finished his sometimes subtle, always powerful, satirical, often ruthless social commentary in seven chapters on the ethics of the upper class and rulers of the *past* compared to the *present* hypocritical, back-stabbing, selfish, treacherous times, one of his masterpieces... *The Ethics of the Nobles*. E.G. Browne in his *A Literary History of Persia* (volume 3 page 244) calls this work "... a very bitter satire on the morals of his time."

Within a year Pir Husain returned to help out his cousin Sheikh Hasan Kuchek defeat Hasan Borzorg in Tabriz who returned his help with an army to take back Shiraz and joining this army was that of the dangerous Mubariz Muzaffar of Yazd who now had eyes for the main prize, Shiraz... and the whole of Fars.

With Pir Husain gone Princess Jahan's father Masud Shah simply marched back into Shiraz and resumed his rulership. But his ease did not last long. On hearing of the size of the armies of Pir Husain and Mubariz that were heading for Shiraz he fled to Baghdad and took refuge with Hasan Borzorg.

The Shirazis fearing the vengeance of Pir Husain and the reputation of the ferocious Mubariz Muzaffar closed the gates and held out bravely against the huge armies for fifty days! Knowing they could not last much longer and their opponents had fared worse than they thought they would, the people called on their revered chief-judge Majd al-Din Isma'il to leave the city and broker a peace with the invaders. This he wisely did to everyone's advantage gaining a promise from Pir Husain to overlook the city's previous relationship to him and to act kindly towards its people. Pir Husain rewarded Mubariz with the city of Kirman.

Later in 1342 Abu Ishak joined his army in Isfahan with Malek Ashraf's and on hearing of this Pir Husain decided to attack them there but he was beaten, and afraid of Mubariz Muzaffar, he decided to seek refuge with Hasan Kuchek his cousin, who immediately executed him.

On advancing on the now wide-open Shiraz, Abu Ishak convinced Malek Ashraf to let him enter the city first where the Shirazis embraced him and took up arms against Ashraf attacking his camp by night and sending his men packing. While this was happening, unbeknownst to Abu Ishak his remaining brother, Jahan's father Masud Shah had entered into a pact with a Chupani commander Amir Yaghibasti (Malek Ashraf's uncle!) and had entered Shiraz. Abu Ishak immediately yielded to the rightful claim of his older brother and left.

Now was Jahan's chance to approach her father about re-appointing Hafiz as her poetry teacher. He agreed as did Hafiz who weekly went to the palace to give her lessons and their budding friendship began to bloom as did the interest in her of Obeyd and her in the crazy poet, joke-teller and unofficial Court jester.

But the situation was soon to change again! Yaghibasti, like Pir Husain before him couldn't bear sharing power and on a fateful day in 1342 as Masud Shah left his bath Yaghibasti had some of his men stab him to death. On hearing of this treachery Abu Ishak was soon to react. He contacted many of the nobles, guild-masters, gang bosses and neighborhood leaders who agreed to join forces with his men by opening the gates to them and attacking Yaghibasti in brawls that lasted in the streets of Shiraz for twenty days! Once again, the Shirazis had been underestimated by a ruler. It is most likely that Hafiz, Jahan who had left the palace on the death of her father and Obeyd all joined in the fighting.

Soon the ruler of Kazerun joined his forces with Abu Ishak's... Yaghibasti and his soldiers fled. Incredibly, a year later Yaghibasti and Malek Ashraf united their armies with Mubariz Muzaffar's and murdered and pillaged their way towards Shiraz, but... upon hearing of the death of the head of the Chupanid family, Hasan Kuchek, the two Chupanids stopped their advance and headed for Tabriz and possible power there and Mubariz, disappointed, returned to Yazd.

So, in 1343 the talented, brave, handsome, youngest brother, Abu Ishak, the son of the much-revered Tashi Khatun, the beloved step-mother of Jahan, to whom Nabat had been promised in marriage but whom she rejected (having fallen in love with Hafiz) now had undisputed power in Isfahan and Shiraz and would do so for most of the next ten amazing years.

During the reign of Pir Husain Jahan had renounced her status of royalty and had lived the life of an ordinary Shirazi and had loved the freedom and liberating effect on her as a woman of the upper class. She had frequented and drunk in many of the winehouses run by the Zoroastrians and Christians and was treated as an equal by the dozens of poets, minstrels and musicians of the city who performed there. They included the now-popular Hafiz, Obeyd, Haydar, Ruh Attar, Junaid Shirazi and a recent arrival from Baghdad and Yazd the famous Court poet Khaju Kirmani who soon, much to the chagrin of Obeyd, became Abu Ishak's official Court poet, while Obeyd had to be content with being a jester again, who delivered satire, obscene jokes and an occasional mystical ghazal.

A controversy at this time was sparked when the poet Haydar accused the Court poet Khaju of plagiarizing the poetry of the immortal poet of Shiraz, Sadi... with this verse...

Eternal... became the life of Sadi,
and love... is the religion of Sadi.
Speakers can't be eloquent when
They are confronted by our... Sadi.

With poems he blazes far horizons:

west, east eclipsed... order of Sadi.

A master of poetry you'll become...

if following foundation set by Sadi.

And if you want to know the truth

love's reason is to be found in Sadi.

All the people... even religious ones

were perplexed because of our Sadi.

My heart, if you want to reach him

In love's faith be sacrificed for Sadi.

To poet don't say " Khaju Kirmani"

for he stole from Divan of our Sadi.

In poetry he can't compete with me,

he dare compare himself with Sadi?

None may be joking except for a fly:

who eats candy from table of Sadi?

Haydar sacrifices himself once, he's

unworthy: thousand times for Sadi!

Obeyd was obviously not enamoured of Khaju but it seems he liked Haydar even less as he states in this poem...

That one, Shahab al-Din Haydar, my brother is...

looking an ass he is really a dog: he's some other?

It's been said that I keep talking about him... but,

if you look, see, it's something... something other.

Someone asked me recently... "Who is that
man?"

"An ugly little man," that was my instant answer.

Hard-on like a donkey's... up gourd of his woman!

A man who's real, goes back on his word? Never!

Obviously at this time in Shiraz under the benign ruler-
ship of Abu Ishak (a fellow-poet and imbiber of wine and
much more) the give and take between the various poets
vying for recognition by the public and the nobles and royalty
was a vigorous affair!

One of the greatest influences on Obeyd and Jahan at
this time and before this time was the infamous female poet
Mahsati (see above) who specialized in the ruba'i and lived
in Ganjeh in the 12th century during the time of Nizami. She
was notorious for her liberated views and actions but
especially for her 'obscene' ruba'is that appealed to Obeyd
who composed many of his own.

Abu Ishak re-appointed as chief minister the wise and
wealthy and respected Khwaja Haji Kivam who soon made
it clear to the young ruler that Hafiz's brilliance in Koran

studies entitled him to teach the same at Kivam's college. Hafiz was summoned to Court and Abu Ishak was amused to see that the man who had won the heart of the most beautiful woman in Shiraz who had been promised to him was small and ugly, but he befriended him immediately... they had much in common, both knew the Koran by heart, both were poets and lovers of beauty.

Meanwhile Obeyd, still infatuated with Jahan kept sending her *ghazals* proclaiming his love and suffering.

Many of Princess Jahan's poems from now on were about one who was to become really the first and great tragic love of her life... the newly appointed minister of Abu Ishak, a brilliant, handsome but vain and womanizing young man from Jahrum, south-east of Shiraz... Amin al-Din Jahrumi. She was besotted by him and his long black hair from the moment he first appeared at Court...

My beloved, why in such a vile way keep treating me:
for God's sake tell me why do you treat me so badly?
Please do not be any worse to me any more than now:
I've lost all patience grieving over you, can't you see?
Our grief is killing us... don't let it exceed its bounds:
what is the full extent of the bounds of your cruelty?

I'm in love with your long, black hair falling in braids:

this deserves, that not broken is your promise to me.

I'll go off and start painting my face with my blood,

because... my beloved, you I can't find and can't see.

If someone other than me you happen to be choosing,

I'd still not find another but you to love... obviously.

I told the breeze of your lips and your beautiful hair...

because I want that breeze to bring your smell to me.

I didn't know that caught in the net of your black hair,

I... not being able to love anyone except you, would be.

Thank God that you keep staying in the world, Jahan,

sometimes you can help any poor beggar that you see.

Jahan's name means 'the world' and in many of her *ghazals* and other poems she uses a play on it or uses it as a double-meaning.

The situation at Court with her displays of love-madness due to her fascination with the uninterested Amin al-Din began to create such a scandal that soon all of Shiraz was talking about her and singing her *ghazals* to him that she would openly read out or sing and dance to during the poetry gatherings that Abu Ishak would have every week where Obeyd would out of jealousy satirize her with his obscene verse and Hafiz, Khaju Kirmani and others try to take the attention away from her.

At this grand occasion at the palace of Jahan's wedding all the local poets were of course invited and many read loving poems and minstrels like Hajji Ahmed sung *ghazals* to the young couple. Not so the envious and brave (and perhaps foolish) Obeyd Zakani who was still hopeful that she may have got over her infatuation and continue the affair she had once had with him.

To the amazement and shock of all gathered there he recited this obscene *ruba'i* of his as his marriage present to her husband for all to hear, using a play on the double-meaning of her name as she often did, and joking about the petite Jahan in relation to the large minister...

Minister, the world (Jahan) an unfaithful prostitute, is not?

One of your stature, ashamed of such a prostitute... is not?

Go, find a pussy who to be fitting your size is quite able...

fit, for you, Lord of the world, Jahan... who is minute, is not.

It is said that Amin al-Din was greatly amused but not so Jahan or her uncle who had to wait for the laughter and obscene talk to die down before Obeyd received his rebuke. It would take years before Jahan could forgive him for this offence.

Hafiz had also married and had a child, a son, but still had a relationship of a Platonic nature with his muse Nabat who never married for she had lost her heart to the small, ugly poet and rejected the king, Abu Ishak, who also eventually married and had a son, Ali Sahl, whose life like that of the son of Hafiz and the daughter of Jahan would be a tragic and not a very long one.

Obeyd would also eventually marry and have three children, two sons and a daughter... one of the sons he named Ishak after Abu Ishak.

Abu Ishak turned out to be an ambitious and often erratic ruler. Soon after gaining power he set his sights on Kirman and came into conflict again with his arch-foe the brave and brutal Mubariz Muzaffar of Yazd who was now ruling there. In 1345 and a year later he attempted unsuccessfully to take the city. Later in the decade he attacked Kirman again then Yazd but failed both times at a great cost, not only to the city coffers but to his own sanity. He seemed to be suffering from paranoid-schizophrenia and this led to bouts of terrible depression or exaggerated pleasure-seeking in wine and women and feasting. The parties at the palace became famous for their wildness and long duration and the false Sufis Shaikh Ali Kolah and the false ascetic Abdullah bin Jiri and their thousands of blue-robed followers began to denounce him and what they saw as Shiraz's lawlessness and contempt for 'Islamic ways'. Obeyd would eventually have his way with them in his outrageous *Tarji Band* or strophe poem *The Book of Masturbation* (see full poem below).

Abu Ishak was too frightened to reign them in and they began to act like a religious police force against the *rinds* and open-minded poets and musicians and Hafiz, Jahan and Obeyd warned of their growing influence. They built a high tower in the city they hypocritically called 'The Tower of Unity' on which they could spy on the population.

During Abu Ishak's open-minded reign the winehouses that were run by the Christians and Zoroastrians flourished and it was there and at Court that Obeyd did his stand-up comic routine (he really was the Lenny Bruce, Robin

Williams, Seinfeld and Eddie Murphy of his time). Many of the ribald stories and obscene jokes that he would soon publish in his *The Joyous Treatise* were first tried out when his fellow poets read there poems at Court and in the winehouses to enthusiastic patrons.

Some years before this was finished he would also complete his controversial *Book of the Beard...* somewhat in the style of Sadi's *Gulistan*. Hasan Javadi in his *The Ethics of the Aristocrats and Other Satirical Works* (pages 22-23) says of it... "...a fantastic dialogue between Obeyd and the beard considered as the destroyer of youthful beauty. The style of Obeyd is both beautiful and skilful... 'The Book of the Beard' mainly dwells on the subject of homosexuality... 'The Book of the Beard' is a light-hearted and witty treatment of the subject, and Obeyd's recommendation is: 'before the calamity of the beard' strikes, make the best use of your time."

During 1350 a biting satire of Obeyd's made its appearance, his *A Hundred Maxims,* that tongue-in-cheek but with his rapier wit, he tore through the hypocrisy of just about all classes in Shiraz and all of Iran at that time and it remains relevant today.

In 1351 with Khaju Kermani sick and out of favour at Court (he would die a year later) Obeyd made another move for becoming the Court poet. He composed and dedicated to Abu Ishak his epic (700 couplets) on human love in *masnavi* form (rhyming couplets) with inserted *ghazals*... *The Book of Lovers.* "It is evidently inspired by the *mathnavi* of the same name by 'Iraqi (d.1289), but in contrast to the latter is written in a mundane mood: we find the customary amorous yearning, finally the visit of the Beloved to the Lover (the poet), separation and thenceforth only yearning for evermore." Jan Rypka (ibid. page 272).

But Abu Ishak had more to think about at this time than Obeyd's hopeful offering. His paranoia extended to the people of Shiraz even though they had fought alongside him many times to rid the city of tyrants. He was afraid they would rise up against him and so prohibited the owning of arms except by his Isfahani soldiers and guards. The people began to resent him. His prime-minister Khwaja Haji Kivam tried to reason with him but insanely again he attacked Yazd and this was the last straw as far as Mubariz was concerned, noting that Abu Ishak had broken eight peace agreements with him. Abu Ishak as a last ditched attempt to stave off an invasion sent one of his minister's as a peace envoy but the scene was set for a final confrontation.

Obeyd could prophesize what would soon happen and did in his next masterpiece... an epic *qasida Mouse and Cat,* that has wrongfully been called a *masnavi* (even though the first two couplets are in *masnavi* form, rhyming separately... in fact it has the same rhyme running all the way through it.

He most likely performed it for the king of the 'mice' Abu Ishak and his small son, the tragic Prince Ali Sahl, who was later to be left behind by his fleeing father then ordered to be killed by the 'cat' Mubariz Muzaffar.

He would end this story of what would shortly occur with these words to his special audience...

This is a tale that is curious and it is strange...

a souvenir from a writer of tales, Obeyd Zakani.

So, dear heart, the moral of this tale please take

and all your days you will live them happily...

upon hearing this ballad of the mouse and cat,

my dear boy, its real meaning... now try to see!

A whole essay could be written on the influence of this long poem on Iran and the rest of the world over the past 600 years and many probably already have. I read once where a commentator stated that the cartoon *Tom and Jerry* was influenced by it! It is possible. It is generally believed now that the tale is about the events that were soon to follow and that the hypocritical cat was Mubariz and the ambitious mouse-king Abu Ishak.

"How deeply he was rooted in the minds of the people is evident from his semi-satirical, semi-comical miniature epic poem *Mush u gurba*, 'Mouse and Cat', that probably had highly political significance. This work is still being widely read in primitive lithographs today." Jan Rypka (ibid 273).

"Suffice to say that the chief concern of Obeyd, as I see it through this satire, is to warn that a free society cannot survive by its wits or by its weapons exclusively, nor even together if the people have lost the will to defend their rights and freedoms." Mehdi Nakosteen, *A Tale of Cats and Mice of Obeyd of Zaakan.* (Introduction).

In 1352 from Kirman and Yazd the tyrant Mubariz brought troops together and marched on Shiraz where Abu Ishak was now drunk most of the time. The terrible siege of the city lasted six months and it was mainly the starving people that held off the dreaded foe. The neighbourhood chiefs and mob bosses were really the ones in charge of the defenses and when Abu Ishak made the mistake of planning to execute one of them for something imagined the district's boss out of self-preservation contacted Mubariz and opened a gate for his troops to enter.

During the siege Khwaja Haji Kivam died and at the end of it in 1353 Jahan's husband, Amin al-Din, fled through one of the *qanats* with Abu Ishak who in his haste to escape left his small son Ali Sahl behind... who was eventually captured and cruelly put to death by Mubariz as was his wife and daughters, and as were many of Shiraz's courageous citizens. The raping, killing and pillaging lasted for weeks.

When the cat saw the king of all of the mice
he boiled with anger, like a cauldron, bubbly!
Strong as a lion and kneeling upon one knee
with teeth he tore the threads and he was free!
He grabbed mice, smashed them into the earth
so that mixed with dirt, them you couldn't see!
The army of mice ran madly in one direction,
king of the mice ran in the other, haphazardly.
The elephant and the elephant rider had fled:
the treasure, crown, throne, palace no longer be!

Abu Ishak and his entourage fled to Isfahan where he began to gather a new army to take back the city but a year later Mubariz's sons laid siege to that city and he was brought back and executed in May 1356 in much style in front of Shiraz's leading citizens (Hafiz and Jahan would have witnessed it) on the steps of the main building at Persepolis. His final words were the following *ruba'i* (sadly, the only one that he is remembered for)…

No hope in family or stranger does remain,

the bird of life now has not a single grain…

all that we said throughout our life is gone,

nothing will survive us, but an echo, vain!

Obeyd would compose this *ghazal* about his old friend and sometimes patron and his reign and eventual fate…

Now see the game… that with him the world did play:

how a disaster took the reins of his happy reign… away.

Such a sea of calamity all of a sudden began to rage and

engulfed his throne, treasures, his son: nothing did stay!

Maybe it was the tears, grief… and fires of many sighs

the palace brought out, caused that house to burn away.

That pleasure-garden whose fine scents and rare colours

were compared to the sacred gardens of paradise, now lay

in such a state… that the nightingale lives there no more,

because the crow with the black heart, has come to stay.

The palace from which Fortune sought some of its wealth

became an owl's nest… a place for dogs to breed and lay!

Obeyd, about the works time brings and the world's state

of come and of go… a thousand gleanings come your way.

As soon as the stern, strict religious fanatic Mubariz Muzaffar had entered the city Shaikh Ali Kolah and his followers had rushed to his side and offered their services in closing the winehouses and brothels and drug dens and policing Islamic law on the point of death.

Obeyd fearing the worst and knowing he would be one of the first to be hunted down, having satirized Mubariz and often Ali Kolah, fled the city with his wife and children in the first week's confusion of murder and plunder and headed in the direction of Baghdad, spending years wandering he would finally arrive there.

I'm leaving the land of Shiraz as my life will be taken…

O, because of this unavoidable despair, heart is broken.

I go, beating head with my hands, feet sinking in shit:

what's to happen to me, on this road what will happen?

Now, I cry out like the nightingale that is lost in love…

now, like the heartsick bud, my collar's been torn open.

I leave this city I'm leaving what I have for an unknown

when I go through the city gate... my life it is gone then.

As I leave my Self, heart, friends, Shiraz behind me...

I go on, hopelessly looking back, remembering... when.

There is no strength in my hands left to hold the reins...

can legs go on when strength from them has been taken?

I'm so sick today and heart-aching from the pain of love:

no help wise friends, parents' advice I should've taken.

O Obeyd, this is not a journey that I wanted to make...

Sky pushes me, then the chain of Fate pulls me... again.

Mubariz's son Shah Shuja who had taken control by blinding and imprisoning his father who cut off the heads of hundreds while holding the *Koran* in one hand and his sword in the other was a liberated ruler in the style of Abu Ishak. He loved poetry and was a fine poet and immediately opened the winehouses and drew poets to his Court from all over Fars. But even the requests of Hafiz and other Shirazi poets to free the tragic and mourning Princess Jahan fell on deaf ears with him for like his father he knew that she may become the focal point of unrest if she was returned to the people who loved her so much. But, under his rule that continued for most of the years from 1358 until 1384 (his brutal Mubariz-like brother Shah Mahmud deposed him for two years, 1364-6) he allowed her to appear at more functions in the palace to recite her poems and occasionally converse with her friends and in particular her mentor, Hafiz.

On his eventual arrival in Baghdad Obeyd discovered that like in Shiraz where the Court poet was Khaju Kermani, Sultan Uvays had a long established Court poet in the famous and accomplished Salman Savaji (1300-76).

Some years previously Salman who had not met Obeyd but had read his works had composed the following poem about him that had been widely circulated throughout the lands...

Obeyd Zakani, the versifier, whose damn pen dripping satire

has made him cursed before God and has all mankind's ire...

he's a stupid bumpkin from the country not a Qazwini at all,

though him, and not without a reason, a 'Qazwini' they call!

The legend is that they met on the banks of the Tigris where Salman was surrounded by many of the city's poets and nobles at a picnic and Salman composed the following line of poetry...

With drunken fury and great frenzy, fiercely the Tigris flows this year...

He turned to the throng gathered around him and asked any of them to finish it. None could, so then Obeyd offered him the line...

with lips spitting foam and chained by feet, it's obviously acting queer.

Salman was impressed and asked Obeyd where he came from. Obeyd said... "Qazvin."

Salman then asked if his own name or poetry is known in Qazvin.

Obeyd answered: '*This,* is famous there...

I'm one who often goes to winehouses and I am a lover of wine,

drunk with drink and desire... at the old Zoroastrian's shrine.

From shoulder to shoulder among them I go like flagon is passed, and from one hand to another hand... like a cup or glass is passed.

Obeyd continued... "As you know, Salman, you are a fully-rounded man (in more ways than one) and these two couplets many think you composed, but it's my opinion they were most likely the creation of your wife, for is not she known to let herself be passed around whenever she gets drunk?"

Salman then asked if he was Obeyd Zakani, and Obeyd confirmed his suspicion then applied to him his cleverest invective finishing with the following words, "You profess, O great Salman, to cultivate erudition and the liberal sciences, but what proofs do you give of this in lampooning a man whom you've never seen, with those whose merits or imperfections you were totally unacquainted and one who has never given you any reason to be displeased with. Your temerity and injustice have induced me to undertake a journey from a distant city to Baghdad solely for the purpose of chastising you. I wished to have met you in the presence of your sovereign, that your punishment might have been as public as the illiberal provocation that caused it. Your good fortune has saved you from that exposure, by throwing you into my claws here on the banks of the Tigris, but I trust that you'll profit by the lesson you've received!"

Although smarting from Obeyd's attack on him he deeply apologized and made him most welcome and Obeyd was given everything he wanted.

But most of Obeyd's years ten years spent back in Baghdad were unsuccessful and blighted by poverty...

In my house, from what's good or bad, there's nothing

except a drug or two, rug old and sad, there's nothing.

Only thing that's cooked up there is a lot of moaning:

other than arse-kick, food to be had... there's nothing!

He would state his own inner condition at the time and criticize Salman's quest for more material riches in the following *ghazal*...

Pain has gone beyond a limit and to remedy we don't come:

soul is to lip, but to Soul of souls, obviously we don't come.

Do those travelling reach the Kaaba... their destination?

To anything but acacia... sharp and thorny, we don't come.

In the Place of Union they live and it's there that they stay:

though we keep trying, to where we journey we don't come.

From incense comes the scent... however to the soul of ours,

that to which acts of ascetics comes easily: we don't come.

Like the mornings breathing purity we breathe in honesty:

it so happens that to Sun shining radiantly, we don't come.

We do not follow Salman in seeking the riches of the world:

and in ways of a king, to Solomon's dignity we don't come.

Exactly like Obeyd we cry: "O God!" from bewilderment...

to the Residency of God's Place of Secrecy, we don't come.

Back in Shiraz Hafiz and Jahan's problems were even worse. Hafiz was self-exiled for a number of years in Isfahan in the late 1360's because of the false rumours and threats of

Shaikh Ali Kolah and certain members of the clergy whom he had openly criticized. Jahan was still under 'house-arrest' at the palace as being the last of the Injus there was still the fear that the Shirazis may rally around her if she was given complete freedom. Both her poems (she composed many hundreds of *ghazals* and *rubais* in prison) and those of Hafiz and Obeyd by this time had become more spiritual and God-absorbed.

O God, from what has happened to Your Grace, we have turned:

hoping for Your Generosity, to Your Path... face we have turned.

From that sick teacher, that old carnal self... Satanic in its ways,

for pardon and protection from what does debase, we have turned.

From the sins we have committed, although we're only to blame,

now that it has turned sallow... to crying, our face we have turned.

Although our book is the blackest that there is, please forgive...

that Book blackened our face and from disgrace... we have turned.

Like Obeyd, we seek Your forgiveness. Unless we turn out to be

completely empty-handed: then to sin to embrace, we have turned.

1365 found Obeyd at the Court of Shah Shuja in Kirman (his brother Mahmud had ousted him from Shiraz). Shuja soon marched on Shiraz and took it back, bringing the aging, sick poet with him. His reunion in Shiraz with Hafiz and the other poets there gave Obeyd a new lease on life, but Hafiz soon went into self-exile for some years and he only saw Jahan when she was released to attend palace functions and Shah Shuja's promises to him of a Court position were only partially fulfilled and he had to copy manuscripts on various subjects to make ends meet.

He became poor and sick and by 1371 his time had come but his passing from this world was not without a sense of humour... in fact it was pure 'Obeydian' as E.G. Browne reveals in his *A Year Amongst the Persians* (page 126-7).

"Even when he was on his death-bed his grim humour did not desert him. Summoning successively to his side his two sons (one named Ishak) and his daughter, he informed them, with every precaution to ensure secrecy, that he had left behind for them a treasure which they must seek for on a particular hour of a certain day after his death and burial in a place which he indicated. "Be sure," he added in conclusion, "that you go there at that hour and at no other and above all keep what I have said secret from my other children." Shortly after this the poet breathed his last and when his body had been consigned to the grave and the day appointed for the search had come, each of his three children repaired secretly to the spot indicated. Great was the surprise of each to find that the others were also present and evidently bent on the same quest. Explanations of a not very satisfactory character ensued, and they then proceeded to dig for the treasure. Sure enough they soon came on a large parcel which they eagerly extracted from its place of concealment and began to unfold. On removing the outer covering they found a layer of straw, evidently designed to protect the valuable and perhaps fragile contents. Inside this was another smaller box, on opening which a quantity of cotton-wool appeared. An eager examination of this brought to light nothing but a small slip of paper on which something was written. Disappointed in their search, but still hoping that this document might prove of value, either by guiding them to the real treasure, or in some other way, they hastily bore it to the light and read these words...

God knows and I know and now you know... indubitably, that... not a single coin is possessed... by Obeyd Zakani.

And on his deathbed Obeyd is reported to have composed his last poem (a *ruba'i*) about the physician who had treated him...

To this stupid doctor no one should apply

to be treated... if one doesn't want to die.

Finally the angel of death to him will say:

"That which you sold for years, now buy!"

Selected Bibliography

Obeyd Zakani: The Dervish Joker, A Selection of his Poetry, Prose, Satire, Jokes and Ribaldry, Translations & Introduction by Paul Smith, New Humanity Books, Campbells Creek, 2012.

The Poets of Shiraz, Translations & Introduction by Paul Smith, New Humanity Books, Campbells Creek, 2012.

The Satirical Prose of Obeyd Zakani: Translations & Introduction by Paul Smith, New Humanity Books Campbells Creek, 2012.

Kulliyat (Collected Works) Obeyd-Zakani. Edited with a preface by 'Abbas Iqbal, Tehran, 1963

The Comic Works of Ubayd-i Zakani: A Study of Medieval Persian Bawdy, Verbal Aggression and Satire by Paul R. Sprachman. University of Chicago Degree Dissertation. 1981.

The Ethics of the Aristocrats and Other Satirical Stories. Obeyd-e Zakani. Translated by Hasan Javadi. Jahan Books Co. 1985.

Obeyd Zakani's Mouse & Cat, Translation and Introduction by Paul Smith. New Humanity Books, Campbells Creek 2011.

Rats Against Cats By Ubaid-i Zakani. Translated by Mas'ud Farzaad. Priory Press, London 1944.

Suppressed Persian. An Anthology of Forbidden Literature. Translated with Notes and an Introduction by Paul Sprachman. Mazda Publications. 1995. (Pages 44-76).

Hafiz's Friend, Jahan Khatun: The Princess Dervish Poet. A Selection of Poems from Her Divan. Translated by Paul Smith and Rezvaneh Pashai. New Humanity Books. Campbells Creek. 2005, 2012.

Hafiz of Shiraz by Paul Smith. 3 volumes... (Obeyd is a major character in this long living-biography.) New Humanity Books, Campbells Creek, 2000-10.

Satire in Persian Literature by Hasan Javadi. Associated University Presses. 1988. (See throughout. Very useful.)

A Year Among the Persians. Edward Granville Browne. A & C Black. 1893. Pages 126-7, 131, 551.

TARJI-BAND...

It is time that our work we will now begin again,

go our wicked ways, blaspheme, lies spin again.

We'll rent a house in a street near the wineseller:

to Tartar beauties... bow in prayer to chin, again.

And if this life does not live up to what we want,

hard-on up arse of fate and life and then, in again!

How much longer must we long for a young butt?

For more pussy we a line stand in to get in, again?

If prick or pussy escape our grip this day, we give

up... then we to play with ourselves begin, again.

Dears, sit for as long as you can, for in this world

nothing can beat doing this self-discipline, again.

Go, let us all masturbate for it's fun to be a jerker:

it's so nice pulling off under the old woolen khirka!

No silver? Nothing happens... no work's finished!

In love's path silver is that one that is way ahead.

There is no big fellow who'll for nothing lie down,

seeking a whore going for free is downright stupid!

And if one doesn't spend what one has saved then

fate just might turn and make off with it instead.

So, go sit down for some time beside a gentle Sufi,

and get some help for your heart that is troubled.

From those cunts and arses take no more trickery:

they'll never give you what's wanted in your head.

So stick it up that unfaithful fool lusting for arse,

and infuriate a dick-head who fucks a girl instead.

Go, let us all masturbate for it's fun to be a jerker:

it's so nice pulling off under the old woolen khirka!

From Kalmuk lands we are, we're crude and tough:

thieving gang of outlawed vultures, mighty rough.

We're devising deeds with beauties day and night,

months... years with lovers we try to get enough.

We'd happily give life for sugar-lipped beauties...

for jasmine-thighed boys, out our souls we'd snuff.

All those boring preachers we are out to destroy:

double-faced false shaikhs, teachers of fake stuff!

We've kissed goodbye the pussy and the arsehole,

although going without them could be quite tough.

O brother, hear me now even if you've half a brain,

this jerk-off offers advice that's still timeless stuff:

go… let us all masturbate for it's fun to be a jerker,

it's so nice pulling off under the old woolen khirka!

All day and night around the city we go carousing,

looking here, there for another who wine's making.

Such drunken fools are we, fearless and full of life:

loving moon-faced beauties, atrociously behaving!

Their curls like lassoes tie our hearts and minds…

their eyebrow-bows our bodies have been striking.

To time's cruelty we pay no heed… we're immune,

free from malicious and evil days… we keep living.

No pussy or arse? We are never afraid or worried

for we're outsiders with arms that are never tiring.

So sit on down and that big thing quickly pull out,

then jerking off all us will keep on happily singing:

go, let us all masturbate for it's fun to be a jerker…

it's so nice pulling off under the old woolen khirka!

My love, pain… world-weariness lasts how long?

That suffering for us, in the past does now belong.

Go, wash your hands free of fortune's evil ways...
and beware of an ambush of time's lurking throng.
Arsehole... pussy, are what? Two holes expelling
waste: one's full of shit, other's stink is too strong.
Give up both of them and go live the life of a hero,
by doing that, kids... wife won't be coming along.
The moment that you notice your prick start rising
if you want to keep your dignity... this do lifelong:
sit down, lick your hands and all of the doors shut
when possible and like Sufi whores, headstrong...
go! Let's all masturbate for it's fun to be a jerker:
it's so nice pulling off under the old woolen khirka!
If possible, go... live the life of a drunken outsider
carousing and whoring in winehouse without fear.
Never throw back a cup without bells and *tanboor*
and only of wine sold by the Magi be the drinker.
O happy, so happy is that one who is inebriated...
not giving a flea's fart about his drunkard's career.
Even if whores and large boys are giving it for free,
for such a one those cunts and arses are a disaster!

So don't go off whoring again, seeking out pussy,

and don't be worrying about any arse's hole either.

Be done with them and each breath will be joyful

then like the masses and also the drunken outsider

go, let us all masturbate for it's fun to be a jerker:

it's so nice pulling off under the old woolen khirka!

So give us wine of the Magi... nothing else will do,

and no other story but of love, tell to me and you.

Do not sit down again beside whatever is horrible:

"Go stand around winestore," advice that is true.

Do not complain again about ruthlessness of fate

and do not expect loyalty from time towards you.

We'll be laughing, drinking and living like royalty

and fart upon beards of you critics... if we want to.

Gentle breeze, from you I'm now needing a favour,

please travel quickly, I am begging you... fly true:

go and search out that boring preacher of this city

then tell to him this, what Obeyd wants you to...

go: let us all masturbate for it's fun to be a jerker...

it's so nice pulling off under the old woolen khirka!

GHAZAL...

Last night your red lips brought a breath so refreshing:
if eyes saw your face, my heart away would be fainting.
Your face, so beautiful, is reminding one of the moon:
long curls of your waving hair with wind, is wrestling.
Your long... your gypsy hair wandering every moment,
in the uneasy hearts of lovers... unease is easily stirring.
Long waving, stirring curls dancing in the moonlight...
heart became like a horse's shoe in a forge, smouldering!
Like daggers... dagger after dagger stuck into my heart:
then the blood of my heart, in rivers of ecstasy gushing.
Your beauty-spot and your lips and your eyes and face:
anyone who saw, or who'd kissed... would be swooning.
Obeyd's eyes that cry blood because they'd seen you...
watch your beautiful face: from eyes tears keep flowing.

RUBA'IS...

Through the bazaar I often go for a walk...
and from their nests see what I can stalk;
perhaps bring a whore home or buy a boy:
either, who cares, anyway it's not for talk.

My prick, that'll beat a minaret even with its large head,

hundreds of husbands for wives would make drop dead...

when into sight a pussy, like a Tartar, comes into view...

it will stand politely, come to it and bow its head instead!

In my prick… a fiery passion boldly grows.

To slow it… its head on my knee it throws.

I'll take it to a pussy-well for there is a deep

spring, next to a wind-shaft that… blows!

The arsehole said: "No other right has the prick

than itself only into pussy, it's allowed to stick!"

Pussy said: "Go away… stop taking such crap!"

"If crap, do you think to keep saying it I'd stick?"

From this furnace, feverish is this prick of mine...

it has become drunk, having sipped a pure wine:

through pussy's path I'll come to a secret place...

that dark, high place... so cool, so moist, so fine!

QIT'AS...

When from a distance women are able see my prick
it's like all their prayers, love letters, are answered!
And when this prick of mine I put into their pussies,
their troubles end: it's like a key a lock has entered!

A good pussy into a person's hands did lay

and he would fuck it every night and day:

when that prick again stiff would become,

from mouth of poor girl's pussy did come...

"At least it's a good thing for me to know

a hopeful one's desires... come and grow!"

O friends, the prick there to be played with...

is not!

Another, of mine a bigger length and width...

is not!

My prick is rising like a flag like any man's would...

a difference between us and king's monolith...

is not!

I take my prick near an arse bent over, for comfort...

for obviously then, pussy coming... forthwith,

is not!

So jerk off, for jerking off is such a good thing to do:

nicer than that... under covers, oneself with,

is not!

My prick mentioned as a fart did leave my arse:

"A scent of the Mulian River

comes this way!"

And when that 'scent' came to me I said this…

"Thought of friend, kind giver,

comes this way."*

*Note: This poem is a send-up of a famous and much-loved poem by the 'Father of Persian Poetry' Rudaki (d. 940). See my 'Rudaki: Selected Poems', New Humanity Books, 2012.

This withered old prick of mine... needs some fresh pussy:

all these old, tattered and battered ones are no good for it!

I ask the Almighty for just one thing... a nice young virgin:

grace can bring it to my door... it's a possibility... isn't it?

Then it may be able to the occasion, do its duty like a man,

and to untie knot of our difficult difficulty... it can see, fit.

PROSE

A king had three wives... a Persian, an Arab and a Coptic wife. One night he slept with the Persian and said 'What time is it?' She answered, 'It's almost morning!' 'How could you possibly know?' he asked. 'Because the smells of the flowers and grasses fill the air and birds sing, sire,' she answered. The next night he asked his Arab wife the same question and she replied, 'Morning's almost here because my necklace's beads are cold and they are making me cold.' On the third night he asked his Coptic wife and she answered, 'It's morning as I've got to go to have a piss!'

Someone asked a slave girl, 'Are you a virgin?' She answered, 'May the Almighty forgive all my sins, I was.'

One man happened to come upon another man fucking his slave girl so he asked her, 'Why did you let that happen?' She replied, 'Master, that man swore to me by your dear head to fuck me, and you know how much I love you... I couldn't refuse him, or else!'

A woman said to her husband, 'You are nothing but a penniless pimp!' He answered her, 'Praise God, that's not my fault. The former is His fault and the latter yours!'

It was the month of Ramadan and a young homosexual was asked if business was slow and he replied, 'It is, but may God keep alive the Christians and Jews!'

The vein of a noble woman was being opened by a blood-letting doctor and when she would ask about any sickness she had he kept saying it was due to too much blood and when finally his knife went into her she let fly a loud fart then asked that doctor, 'Was that because of too much blood?' He answered, 'No from too much widening of the arsehole!'

There was a married woman who had a lover who was named Muhammad and he was a tailor. Her husband told her one day. 'I wish to bring some friends home tomorrow so tell me anyone else you think would also be a welcome guest.' She answered, 'That tailor named Muhammad would be fine.' So he was invited as well and when they'd all finished eating the fine spread in the garden Muhammad went into the house and found the wife to amuse him. The husband heard them at it and rushed into the room and tried to grab him but could only snatch hold of his penis but as it was wet it eventually slipped from his hand and Muhammad managed to escape. When he got back to his house his wife was indignant and refused to speak to him. He said to her, 'My dear wife, what sin is it that I have done that you should act like this towards me? I allowed him to come here as you asked me to and I fed him. You had sex with him then I cleaned his penis and I accompanied the man all the way to the safety of his house. If I have not played my part please tell me how so I can offer my apologies and if you know of any other service I can do please tell me what it is so I can rise to the occasion!'

There was a very important man who had a very beautiful wife whose name was Zohreh and one day he had to make a trip, so he organized to have a white dress made for her and then he gave to one of his slaves a bowl of dye made of indigo and said to him, 'If ever the my wife should do some indecent act then you place a finger of this dye upon her dress so that after I come back if you're not present I'll know what has been going on!' Sometime later that important man wrote a couplet to his slave that read…

Has Zohreh done anything that's dark,
leaving upon her dress an indigo mark?
That slave of his answered with another…

If my master delays his return any further,

your beloved Zohreh will become a zebra!

There was a judge who had bad colic and the doctor mentioned to his family that they should give him an enema... with wine. So they took his advice and poured much wine into him and of course he became drunk and then he got up and began to beat up his family and shouting. Someone asked his son, 'What's your father doing?' And his son replied, 'From the bottom of him comes a riot!'

A woman had already survived two husbands and he third was near death and as she cried she asked him, 'My dear, where do you go and who do you give me to be looked after by?' He replied, 'The fourth cuckold!'

There was a woman who sat next to her lover while a preacher delivered a sermon and as he talked about Gabriel's wings she tossed the corner of her veil over her lover's knees and touched him and soon he had an erection that made her cry out. That preacher was very happy with her enthusiasm for his words and called to her, 'Did Gabriel's wing reach your soul madam that you let out such a loving sigh?' The woman answered him, 'Gabriel's wing? I have no idea! But Seraphiel's trumpet came to hand and caused me to shout!'

The wife of Maulana Azd al-Din Iji (a great scholar and philosopher of Shiraz d. 1355) gave birth to a son who hadn't an arse-hole and all the doctors couldn't discover a remedy so after a few days the baby died. Azd al-Din cried, 'Almighty God! I've been looking for fifty years but have never found an arse whole, except for his, but he died within three days!'

A woman with her son was held up by a Turk in the middle of nowhere. He raped both of them and then disappeared. The woman turned to her son and asked, 'If you saw him again would you know him?' He replied, 'He faced you, so you're more likely to know him!'

A man got married and on the night of his wedding he went out to do something and after he came back he noticed that his bride had taken a needle and was piercing her ears. While they were making love later he found out she wasn't a virgin. Angrily he shouted at her, 'My dear, those holes you should've made when you were in the house of your father you're making here and the one you should've made here has been made in your father's house!'

A young woman went and complained to a judge that her husband was not giving her what was rightfully hers. Her husband answered, 'I'm doing only what I'm capable of!' She replied, 'I'm not satisfied with any less than five times a night!' He answered, 'I'm not boasting but I can do it three times a night.' The judge said, 'There's really no problem between you if I do something about it, I'll do the other two times a night!'

A man said to a beautiful woman that he came across... 'Let me taste you, my dear, and then I'll know if you are any more sweeter than my dear wife.' She answered him... 'Why don't you just go and ask my husband as he's tasted the both of us!'

There was a mature woman who heard a preacher giving a talk. She went home and said to her husband... 'I heard a preacher who said that a house will be built in heaven for one who has sexual intercourse with his lawful wife that very night!' They went to bed later that night and the wife said to him: 'Now you get up if you want a house in heaven.' The man made love once to his wife. Some time went by and she woke him again and said, 'You've built one for you now build one for me.' So he built one more. Some time later she woke him saying, 'What if a guest comes?' So he built a guesthouse. The following morning the husband suddenly grabbed hold of his wife and before she could stop him he fucked her in the arse, saying, 'One who has built three houses in heaven should build at least one down in hell!'

I heard about a member of the nobility whose wife was chaste and ugly. He was able to divorce her and marry a pretty harlot... and when (as was her habit) his new wife invited all others to partake of her generosity, many criticised him for rejecting a chaste woman for a whore. That noble with much patience, unperturbed, answered... 'You fools! Your weak minds can't get the wisdom of my actions. When in the past I was made to nibble alone on those shitty little scraps of my previous wife's favours... now I'm dining on the sweets of my present tempting one along with all the other thousands!'

A Hamadani gentleman was entering his house as a handsome young man was exiting it. He shouted at the young man, 'I curse the kind of life you are leading young man. Why keep going into other people's houses? By God, why don't you get married like others so ten other men can get something out of it?'

A thief made his way into old Robabi's house... but old Robabi was wide awake and in the dark covered the thief's exit with his body crying out for his slave girl, 'O Shadi, come and massage my feet!' The thief had to make out he was Shadi and massaged his feet and old Robabi had an erection and called out, 'O Shadi, let's have sex!' The poor thief had to let Robabi have sex with him. Then Robabi said: 'Let's do it again!' The poor thief had to do it three... four more times! Good grief! Out in the garden was tied up a neighbour's skinny old horse and Robabi shouted: 'O Shadi go and water the horse.' At the well the hole in the bucket meant the thief couldn't give the horse enough water. In the end, after he'd tried the man's patience every way possible, he made out he fell asleep. The thief realised his opportunity and ran off and when he saw some other thieves who were digging a tunnel under the wall into Robabi's house he shouted, 'Don't waste your time there... in there there's nothing valuable. Just an old faggot who's on a sex drug and never gets tired of fucking and a horse with dropsy so bad that all the water in the world won't quench its thirst!'

There was a woman with big beautiful eyes. She went to a judge and brought a charge against her husband. The judge was a woman-chaser and loved her eyes. He wanted her so he sided with her. The husband could see this so he pulled off her veil and the judge looked at her face that *wasn't* very beautiful. 'Get up,' he said, 'woman… you've the eyes of the innocent but the face of the guilty!'

An old faggot said to a boy, 'If you let me fuck you I'll only use half my prick.' The boy consented. The old faggot then added, 'I meant of course the second half of my prick!'

And have you heard about the wife of the Turkoman who while sitting in the water had a lobster attach itself to her pussy? She screamed out from the pain and her husband came running. Now he'd heard that if one blows on the back of a lobster it'll give up whatever it has a hold on. So, he bent down and blew upon the lobster and his wife's pussy… but, suddenly the lobster had hold of his lip with its other claw but the man kept on blowing. All of a sudden his wife farted and his spirits were dampened and he shouted, 'Hey, don't you blow also, your breath stinks!'

On Chastity.

We can read about those most excellent personages of long ago that they then believed that chastity was a virtue to be admired and that it meant that one was unsullied. They saw chastity in one who averted his eyes from certain women who shouldn't be looked at, never listened to slanderous gossip, kept his hands from taking another's goods, never let tongue utter an obscene word and kept his soul far away from whatever was considered worthy of censure! Such a being as this was admired and praised. The poet has expressed this so…

That person, is above all others respected…

who like cypress is dignified, loftily erected.

It's said that once a wise man heard his son abusing, finding fault with another and he said to him, 'Son, why are you happy to pollute your mouth with what you don't like in someone else?' It is also told that when Mansur Hallaj (may Allah sanctify his soul) had been hung on the gibbet he said, 'When I was a boy I walked along a street and listened to the voice of a woman over a fence. To try to see her I looked over. Now my looking down from this position I think is in repayment for that time I looked over!'

And now, *in the present,* our masters consider that those long ago made a terrible mistake in relation to this… and their valuable lives were passed lacking foresight and in total stupidity. They say that anyone who follows chastity's way will get nothing out of this life. It's revealed: '… life of this world is only amusing games, pomposity and bragging to each other and multiplying amongst yourselves and having riches and offspring' (57:20). They take this to mean that in this world life's reason for existing is playing and enjoyment, being vain, trying to gain glory, getting as much wealth as possible and pushing one's family tree as high as possible. Their argument is that because play and any enjoyment without being depraved and any methods of gaining pleasures that are forbidden are impossible… and any gathering of wealth without harming others, terrifying others, tricking and being treacherous towards them and also slandering them isn't possible and one who practices chastity will never gain whatever is the purpose of existence. They *don't* think such a one is really alive and think his existence is a joke and quote the following… 'Do you think that We created you as a joke and that you'd not be brought back to Us' (23:115). What absolute stupidity it would have to be if someone alone with a moon-faced beauty didn't take advantage of an inspiring union with such a vision by claiming that one's chastity meant one couldn't take advantage. It's possible that one would never again have such an opportunity throughout his life and would die of heartache, muttering… 'Such an opportunity wasted leads to heartache!' Such a person who long ago they'd praise as 'chaste, self-restrained, unsullied,' today they'd call 'an idiot, boring and miserable'. They think Allah made eyes, ears, tongues and the body's other organs to make a profit and repulse injury. Denying any organ the only reason for existence means that organ would be gone. And since such a loss of any organ should be avoided all must see what their eyes are happy to see, hear what ears are happy to hear, say whatever is of help to them alone even if spiteful, malicious, hateful, treacherous, deceitful, offensive, obscene or a lie. And if one is injured by this or that one's family is ruined… what's the difference? One should never pay attention to such things and never let them bite one's conscience. Just say and do whatever one wants and fuck who ever you want to or your life will become intolerable…

Those worth finding are those exquisite beauties...

lovers smooth and slim, while you still have abilities:

allow no time for snoring or breathing, when found...

fuck them, finish with them, then for more look around.

These ones also believe that if a companion or master wants pleasure from one, then one should immediately comply and never think to resist because 'opportunities fly away like the clouds'. Or, as Sadi says...

Don't put off today's deed until tomorrow...

you can't know if it will bring joy or sorrow.

And one should never think of saying *no* to an offer because 'to regret is to be impious'. It's much better to see it as a wonderful opportunity, for it has been seen that anyone, woman or man, who hasn't agreed to *do it...* is always unhappy and in agony, burned by deprivation and self-denial. It's absolutely true and has been so, due to incontestable proof, since Adam (peace upon him) walked the earth until this time... that anyone who didn't agree to *do it* never became an *amir,* minister, hero, killer of whole armies, champion, owner of property, favoured by fate, a *shaikh,* preacher, or chief. In support of this is the truth that in Sufism to be fucked is called 'the affliction of the *shaikh'.* It's been written that Rustom, Zal's son, gained such a great reputation and fame because of intercourse of the anus, for as the poets have said...

The moment that Rustom his belt had untied...
this proud hero knelt before Human... waited:
out like a smokestack Human pulled his rod...
in the same way that Godarz ruled... like a god.
He rammed hard into Rustom and harder still...
Rustom's rectum with passion did pulse... until
Human turned around and his big arse did bare,
and like some fierce lion Rustom without a care
speared into Human with a rod hard as a rock...
Human's arse almost in half shuddered in shock.
See how those heroes, backsides worn and tired,
had become the greatest champions... ever sired.
Once you are bigger and stronger, O my brother,
and have the brains to listen to my story longer,
can lay down and show off your arsehole to all,
and let them see how very arsetistic is your hole.
And then, by anybody you meet you'll be fucked,
no longer being in fear of any prick you've sucked.
And from a short stay on this earth you'll know,

better to have left only good behind... then blow!

And of course the wise ones of this age have said this also...

In the gift of pussy there is eternal joy,

that one who gets it is a winning boy!

The experience of our great men obviously confirms this. And of course they have truth on their side because in this world it's quite clear that if one's anus is whole there's no reward. As order in the world comes from give and take then a man must do and also be done to... to be thought of as an eminent person and 'an aristocrat of both directions'. If his mother and father have always let it happen to them then it's correct to call him 'an advantaged two-sided aristocrat'. Although the ordinary folk may jeer that sodomy is back-the-front charity and arse-wise benevolence, whatever they say isn't credible for they don't know the proverb... 'Generosity to yourself is the greatest form of charity'. Those who may be unfortunate enough to miss such an opportunity shall lose the keys to being prosperous and will be stuck forever in misery and humiliation. To benefit these people it is advised...

Regret what you have? So bite your finger!

When the time was ripe... you didn't linger!

To you dear fortunate ones whose minds can accept any good advice... this much on this subject will do. May Almighty God help all of you to do your best.

Our philosophers and scientists say astrology is a misuse of astronomy... as Ibn Sina and Ibn Khaldun pronounced, but what would those two ignoramuses know about it? I say...

After you open up the book to find the omen,

find omen's meaning from Obeyd... O men!

Listen well my friend to these words of wisdom. 'While asleep, news comes that in a particular place they've opened the robe of your son and buggered him! This news is correct... no possibility of falsehood or truth!

'May your beard be farted upon and your moustache be shat on,' and 'You will be occupied for some time with your testicles,' and the second house informs you 'because of being a husband your veiled ones or your wives will have maces placed in them, front and behind, and your store shall be full of that harvest... so give liberally to the poor and gain greater reward'.

'Excrement... shit... will come to you from members of your own family and your brothers will 'on your moustache and your sisters shit, and on your beard... and your cows will fart on your moustache, also so that it will turn white if black and black if white and when you experience having a weak heart your nurses that will fart on your beard, will cure you, but... in order to cure other diseases you will get, you must clean your cows arses with your beard and must keep your moustache far from the pubic hair of nurses, female servants as this will rid you of lice. And... the eleventh house of Gemini will bring the promise of your flatulence which will certainly be fulfilled for you are of a highly auspicious house'.

*

Dear friends, make the best... the most of your life.

Don't waste your precious time.

Don't leave pleasures of today 'til tomorrow.

Don't spoil a good day.

Think of wealth, play and health as the real kingdom.

Enjoy the present... you'll not live again.

If one forgets his origin and status... don't remind him.

Don't welcome anyone conceited.

Don't count sick days among those of your life.

Regard greatly those of high spirits and good natures... people with a dervish-like temperament.

Forget expecting help from others... then you'll happily laugh in their faces.

Don't frequent courts of kings... turn down their rewards so one can avoid their officials.

Sacrifice your life for sake of good friends.

Think of seeing beautiful people as life's happiness... light of eye and joy of heart.

Curse them who raise eyebrows, wrinkle foreheads, talk seriously... have sour faces and those who are bad-tempered, liars, miserly, ill-mannered.

Fart on the beards of the high and mighty and dignified who have no mercy.

As much as you can don't speak the truth, so that you're not a bore to others, causing much annoyance.

Become involved in all kinds of ribaldry, cuckoldry, gossip, ingratitude and false testimony!

Sell heaven for earth and playing the *daf* so you'll become dear to the powerful and so enjoy life.

Don't believe their sermons or you'll stray and end in hell.

If you want to be saved, become a servant of these sacrificing, pure-hearted *rinds*... these 'drunken-outsiders' then you'll be saved.

Don't live in the neighbourhood of these sanctimonious ones so you'll live to your heart's delight.

And don't room in a street of a minaret, so you'll be safe from annoying noise of muezzins.

Help an addict by giving him food and sweetmeats.

Give helping hands to the drunkard.

For as long as you're living... be happy and don't think about all those vulturous inheritors of yours.

Think about being un-attached, a *kalandar*... a dervish... as the foundation of a happy life.

Be free from a good or bad reputation's chains... so you'll live freely.

Don't fall into women's traps... and watch out for widows with brats.

Don't be wasting precious time on lawful... but cold, lovemaking.

Don't marry the daughters of judges, clergy, sheikhs or nobles... and if such a marriage happens against your will, have intercourse with your bride in the backside or the evil from where she came will show itself and your children will be hypocrites, beggars or headaches for you.

Don't marry daughters of preachers... she may give birth to an ass.

Fear this... providing for wet-nurse, philosophising midwives, dominance of pregnant wife, cradle's babble, greeting of son-in-law, duties towards wife... unruliness of children.

Think of masturbation as better than seduction.

Don't expect young women to be friendly to you when you're old.

Don't make love to old women... for nothing!

Don't get married or you might become a pimp.

Beat up old women so you attain status of warrior for the Faith.

Out on the street, don't be deceived by the tall form of veiled women, or... by veils hemmed with brocade.

Take advantage of money and bodies of slaves, so you can be thought of as law-abiding.

Don't leave waiting any instrument of eating and fucking for one moment.

And when you find a pretty boy drunk and asleep, grab that opportunity before they wake.

Extend your sexual help to deserving persons such as secluded women who can't leave houses, old and poor homosexuals, youths whose beards have grown preventing them doing their business and young women with husbands away... as such charity brings blessings.

Don't wine and dine alone as this is what Jews and judges do!

And never ask anything from upstart sons of beggars.

Do buy Turkish slave-boys at any price when they've no beard but sell them at any price when beards grow.

Don't turn your arse away from friends and enemies when young so in old age you can become a sheikh, preacher or a man of name, fame and dignity.

And buy slaves that are soft-handed and not hard-fisted.

Don't ever accept wine from hand of bearded winebringers.

Never expect comfort, peace, blessings in house of a man with two wives.

Chastity... don't expect it from a lady reading Gurgani's romance *Vis and Ramin* and don't expect anal integrity from that boy drinking wine and smoking *bhang*.

But... you *can* have anal intercourse with daughter of your neighbour and don't touch her hymen, then you'll not have betrayed your neighbour and you'll be considerate... a good Muslim. On her wedding night she will not be ashamed before bridegroom and be proud among the people.

In this age don't expect to find an honest governor, a judge not accepting bribes, ascetic who doesn't speak hypocritically, official not corrupt or statesman who preserved *his*... anal integrity.

You want God to be compassionate to you? Be compassionate to young women with husbands away, to lover with beloved first time failing to perform... to a winebringer who goes to parties where some libertine doesn't like him and kicks him out, and to throngs of half-drunken men who've spilt their wine and towards young men in the grip of shrewish wives and girls who have lost their virginity and are terrified of wedding nights fast approaching.

If a woman is on her death-bed fuck her or any others in same situation as this is a great opportunity.

Be content with only dry-humping the young then you'll have been acting kindly towards them.

Don't think of the man who knocks out his opponent as an athlete or a wrestler... but as one placing another's face on floor so he can be mounted.

Don't believe in promises of drunkards, women's flirting, prostitutes vows, a homosexual's flattery.

To your teachers and masters, patrons and partners in bed (of either sex) try to be polite, so you will not be betrayed by them.

Never be upset by beggars curses, women being slapped, sayings of poets and jesters.

Sleep with handsome boys and enjoy it... it's a joy you'll not find in paradise.

In gambling and backgammon use every trick so that you'll be called the perfect gambler. If the opponent questions you, swear that if you're not telling the truth may your wife be completely divorced from you, for such swearing is no sin in gambling.

Don't pay young boys and prostitutes before you're finished so they'll not stop before the climax and there'll be no fight with them.

Never let gabbers, gossipers or the mean into your parties... and no drunkards and no tuneless minstrels who keep repeating their mournful songs.

Stay away from groups of party-goers that love to fight.

Never put a prostitute and pretty-boy in the same place.

Never play backgammon on credit so that you'll have to talk others heads off for nothing.

When taking a young boy to your room be careful... and as he leaves be wary he doesn't steal from you.

Unless food and sweetmeats are placed in front of you, don't smoke any *bhang.*

Meddlers and hung-over party-goers tell to go to hell when next morning they frown your way, blaming you... criticising, declaring that the previous night you were very drunk, broke wine-jugs, gave away money, clothes... so then they won't bother others also.

Women... beat them well and then love them passionately so they'll fear you and be obedient. The master of the house's role can be, through fear and hope, made easier... displeasure can be made into... pleasure.

Use compliments, sweet words... to seduce that one you love.

Don't be drunk near ponds or canals or openings of *qanats*... so you'll not fall in.

Don't converse with shaikhs, those recently come into wealth, fortune-tellers, morticians and aggressive beggars, chess players and lavish spenders, old families descendants or anyone else stricken with such misfortune.

Expect no honesty or fairness or conduct of a good Muslim from anyone in business.

Don't be displeased about the slapping around or robbing of old homosexuals.

And you beware of hypocrisy of judges, the tumult caused by the Mongols, the outrage of pederasts, friendship of those whom you once slept with and are now daring and powerful heroes.

Also beware of poets tongues, women's deceit, jealous ones evil eyes, hatred of relatives.

Expect nothing from a disobedient child, shrewish wife, old lazy horse, servant trying to run you, or useless friends.

Never fart without the right ablution at foot of preacher's pulpit, for it's not authorised by religious scholars long dead.

Realise youth's better than old age, health's better than being sick, wealth's better than poverty, prostitution's better than being a cuckold and drunkenness is better than being sober and wisdom's better than madness.

Never repent or you'll become unfortunate, unlucky, sick and boring.

And never go on the *Hajj* pilgrimage or you might become greedy and faithless.

Don't show your beloved's house to anyone.

And don't make love to women by yourself... this, isn't gentlemanly my friends.

Never fear or be ashamed of becoming a cuckold then you can spend your days without grief and nights without worrying.

Be friendly with winesellers and *bhang*-sellers so you'll insure future pleasures.

Never drink wine before people in Ramadan so they'll never see you as a faithless one.

Don't accept testimony of the blind in Ramadan even if they're on top of a mountain.

And never ask for the poll-tax from shoe-makers, blood-cuppers and weavers... if they're all Muslims.

Don't exaggerate honesty and faithfulness, or you'll become sick with colic and similar illnesses.

Attend early morning *bhang* and wine parties so that fortune will come your way, as everywhere corruption is an omen of good-fortune.

Try sleeping with sons of shaikhs in any way you can because it's thought of as similar to a great pilgrimage.

Never be seen as a generous man in a winehouse, gambling den, or party of whores and pederasts so they'll not come to you for anything.

And don't offer your home to those newly rich... or to upstart sons of slaves or peasants.

Run from being in debt to relatives, misers' tables, grimacing servants, fighting of family members and anyone asking for a loan.

And try to avoid death for it's been hated since the old days.

Please don't throw yourself in a well and injure yourself... unless it's absolutely necessary.

And never listen to words of shaikhs or opium smokers since it's been said...

Whatever wisdom an opium smoker says, you write it

on the prick of an ass, then give it back to him… to fit.

Go and sow your sperm unlawfully so as your children will become theologians, sheikhs and favourites of the king.

Don't hate this ribaldry and don't look down at us satirists.

Listen and make sure you act upon these words as they're words of great men.

Yes, these are sayings that have come down to us from our masters and great men. Those who are ready for such insights may benefit from them, for as it is said by our beloved Sadi…

Fortunate ones to advice always listen closely…
and great men accept dervishes' counsel happily.

May Almighty God open wide the door of happiness, peace and strength… to all of you!

The bachelor... one enjoying the world; the ghoul... a female matchmaker; unfortunate... a householder; two-horned... one having two wives; most unfortunate of unfortunates... he having more than two; cuckold with a sour face... the father-in-law; shrew with a cold heart... mother-in-law; futile... householder's life; wasted... his time; dissipated... his wealth; distracted... the householder's mind; bitter... that one's enjoyment; place of mourning... his house; foe of the family... his son; unlucky... young man with old wife; cuckold; old man with young wife; horned ram... man whose wife reads romance Vis and Ramin; divorce... the cure; joy following sorrow... a triple divorce; love... occupation of those with nothing to do.

The lady... she who has many lovers; the housewife... one who has few; the virtuous... she who's satisfied with one lover; the true lady... she who makes love for free; the charitable... man who makes love to an old lady; the poor... she who courts strangers; the aphrodisiac... leg of someone else's wife; a virgin... name meaning nothing!

BOOKS PUBLISHED BY NEW HUMANITY BOOKS
BOOK HEAVEN

*Most 6" x 9" (15 cm x 23 cm) Paperbacks Perfectbound
unless stated otherwise...
Most also available in pdf format
from: www.newhumanitybooks.com
check out our website for prices & full descriptions of each book.
Also available from Amazon.com
many titles are also in Kindle format e-books*

TRANSLATIONS

*(NOTE: All translations by Paul Smith are in clear, modern English
and in the correct rhyme-structure of the originals and as close to the
true meaning as possible.)*

DIVAN OF HAFIZ
Revised Translation & Introduction by Paul Smith
This is a completely revised one volume edition of the only modern,
poetic version of Hafiz's masterpiece of 791 *ghazals, masnavis, rubais*
and other poems/songs. The spiritual and historical and human content
is here in understandable, beautiful poetry: the correct rhyme-structure
has been achieved, without intruding, in readable (and singable)
English. In the Introduction of 70 pages his life story is told in greater
detail than any where else; his spirituality is explored, his influence on
the life, poetry and art of the East and the West, the form and function
of his poetry, and the use of his book as a worldly guide and spiritual
oracle. His Book, like the *I Ching,* is one of the world's Great Oracles.
Included are notes to most poems, glossary and selected bibliography
and two indexes. First published in a two-volume hardback limited
edition in 1986 the book quickly went out of print. 542 pages.

PERSIAN AND HAFIZ SCHOLARS AND ACADEMICS WHO
HAVE COMMENTED ON PAUL SMITH'S TRANSLATION OF
HAFIZ'S 'DIVAN'.

"It is not a joke... the English version of ALL the *ghazals* of Hafiz is a great feat and of paramount importance. I am astonished. If he comes to Iran I will kiss the fingertips that wrote such a masterpiece inspired by the Creator of all and I will lay down my head at his feet out of respect." Dr. Mir Mohammad Taghavi (Dr. of Literature) Tehran.
"I have never seen such a good translation and I would like to write a book in Farsi and introduce his Introduction to Iranians." Mr B. Khorramshai, Academy of Philosophy, Tehran.
"Superb translations. 99% Hafiz 1% Paul Smith."Ali Akbar Shapurzman, translator of many mystical works in English to Persian and knower of Hafiz's *Divan* off by heart.
"I was very impressed with the beauty of these books." Dr. R.K. Barz. Faculty of Asian Studies, Australian National University.
"Smith has probably put together the greatest collection of literary facts and history concerning Hafiz." Daniel Ladinsky (Penguin Books author of poems inspired by Hafiz).

HAFIZ – THE ORACLE
(For Lovers, Seekers, Pilgrims, and the God-Intoxicated).
Translation & Introduction by Paul Smith. 441 pages.

HAFIZ OF SHIRAZ.
The Life, Poetry and Times of the Immortal Persian Poet.
In Three Books by Paul Smith. Over 1900 pages, 3 volumes.

PIERCING PEARLS: THE COMPLETE ANTHOLOGY OF PERSIAN POETRY
(Court, Sufi, Dervish, Satirical, Ribald, Prison & Social Poetry from the 9th to the 20th century.) Volume One
Translations, Introduction and Notes by Paul Smith. Pages 528.

PIERCING PEARLS: THE COMPLETE ANTHOLOGY OF PERSIAN POETRY
(Court, Sufi, Dervish, Satirical, Ribald, Prison & Social Poetry from the 9th to the 20th century.) Vol. Two
Translations, Introduction and Notes by Paul Smith. Pages 462.

DIVAN OF SADI: His Mystical Love-Poetry.
Translation & Introduction by Paul Smith. 421 pages.

RUBA'IYAT OF SADI
Translation & Introduction by Paul Smith. 151 pages.

WINE, BLOOD & ROSES:
ANTHOLOGY OF TURKISH POETS
Sufi, Dervish, Divan, Court & Folk Poetry from the 12th – 20th Century
Translations, Introductions, Notes etc., by Paul Smith. Pages 286.

OBEYD ZAKANI: THE DERVISH JOKER.
A Selection of his Poetry, Prose, Satire, Jokes and Ribaldry.
Translation & Introduction by Paul Smith. 305 pages.

OBEYD ZAKANI'S > MOUSE & CAT ^ ^
(The Ultimate Edition)
Translation & Introduction etc by Paul Smith. 191 pages.

THE GHAZAL: A WORLD ANTHOLOGY
Translations, Introductions, Notes, Etc. by Paul Smith. Pages 658.

NIZAMI: THE TREASURY OF MYSTERIES
Translation & Introduction by Paul Smith. 251 pages.

NIZAMI: LAYLA AND MAJNUN
Translation & Introduction by Paul Smith. 215 pages.

UNITY IN DIVERSITY
Anthology of Sufi and Dervish Poets of the Indian Sub-Continent
Translations, Introductions, Notes, Etc. by Paul Smith. Pages... 356.

RUBA'IYAT OF RUMI
Translation & Introduction and Notes by Paul Smith. 367 pages.

THE *MASNAVI*: A WORLD ANTHOLOGY
Translations, Introduction and Notes by Paul Smith. 498 pages.

HAFIZ'S FRIEND, JAHAN KHATUN:
The Persian Princess Dervish Poet...
A Selection of Poems from her *Divan*
Translated by Paul Smith with Rezvaneh Pashai. 267 pages.

PRINCESSES, SUFIS, DERVISHES, MARTYRS &
FEMINISTS: NINE GREAT WOMEN POETS OF THE
EAST: A Selection of the Poetry of Rabi'a of Basra, Rabi'a of Balkh,
Mahsati, Lalla Ded, Jahan Khatun, Makhfi, Tahirah, Hayati and
Parvin.
Translation & Introduction by Paul Smith. Pages 367.

RUMI: SELECTED POEMS
Translation, Introduction & Notes by Paul Smith. 220 pages.

KABIR: SEVEN HUNDRED SAYINGS *(SAKHIS)*.
Translation & Introduction by Paul Smith. 190 pages. Third Edition

SHAH LATIF: SELECTED POEMS
Translation & Introduction by Paul Smith. 172 pages

LALLA DED: SELECTED POEMS
Translation & Introduction by Paul Smith. 140 pages.

BULLEH SHAH: SELECTED POEMS
Translation & Introduction by Paul Smith. 141 pages.

NIZAMI: MAXIMS
Translation & Introduction Paul Smith. 214 pages.

KHIDR IN SUFI POETRY: A SELECTION
Translation & Introduction by Paul Smith. 267 pages.

ADAM: THE FIRST PERFECT MASTER AND POET
by Paul Smith. 222 pages.

MODERN SUFI POETRY: A SELECTION
Translations & Introduction by Paul Smith. Pages 249

LIFE, TIMES & POETRY OF NIZAMI
by Paul Smith. 97 pages.

RABI'A OF BASRA: SELECTED POEMS
Translation by Paul Smith. 102 pages.

RABI'A OF BASRA & MANSUR HALLAJ
~Selected Poems~
Translation & Introduction Paul Smith. Pages 134

SATIRICAL PROSE OF OBEYD ZAKANI
Translation and Introduction by Paul Smith. 212 pages.

KHAQANI: SELECTED POEMS
Translation & Introduction by Paul Smith. 197 pages.

IBN 'ARABI: SELECTED POEMS
Translation & Introduction by Paul Smith. 121 pages.

THE *GHAZAL* IN SUFI & DERVISH POETRY:
An Anthology:
Translations, Introductions, by Paul Smith Pages 548.

A GREAT TREASURY OF POEMS
BY GOD-REALIZED & GOD-INTOXICATED POETS
Translation & Introduction by Paul Smith. Pages 804.

MAKHFI: THE PRINCESS SUFI POET ZEB-UN-NISSA
A Selection of Poems from her *Divan*
Translation & Introduction by Paul Smith. 154 pages.

~ THE SUFI RUBA'IYAT ~
A Treasury of Sufi and Dervish Poetry in the *Ruba'i* form,
from Rudaki to the 21st Century
Translations, Introductions, by Paul Smith. Pages... 304.

LOVE'S AGONY & BLISS: ANTHOLOGY OF URDU
POETRY: Sufi, Dervish, Court and Social Poetry from the 16th- 20th
Century Translations, Introductions, Etc. by Paul Smith. Pages 298.

RUBA'IYAT OF ANSARI
Translation & Introduction by Paul Smith. 183 pages

THE RUBAI'YAT: A WORLD ANTHOLOGY:
Court, Sufi, Dervish, Satirical, Ribald, Prison and Social Poetry in the
Ruba'i form from the 9th to the 20th century from the Arabic, Persian,
Turkish, Urdu and English.

Translations, Introduction and Notes by Paul Smith Pages 388.

BREEZES OF TRUTH
Selected Early & Classical Arabic Sufi Poetry
Translations, Introductions by Paul Smith. Pages 248.

THE~DIVINE~WINE:
A Treasury of Sufi and Dervish Poetry (Volume One)
Translations, Introductions by Paul Smith. Pages... 522.

THE~DIVINE~WINE:
A Treasury of Sufi and Dervish Poetry (Volume Two)
Translations, Introductions by Paul Smith. Pages... 533.

TONGUES ON FIRE: An Anthology of the Sufi, Dervish,
Warrior & Court Poetry of Afghanistan.
Translations, Introductions, Etc. by Paul Smith. 322 pages.

THE SEVEN GOLDEN ODES (QASIDAS) OF ARABIA
(The Mu'allaqat)
Translations, Introduction & Notes by Paul Smith. Pages... 147.

THE QASIDA: A WORLD ANTHOLOGY
Translations, Introduction & Notes by Paul Smith. Pages... 354.

IBN AL-FARID: WINE & THE MYSTIC'S PROGRESS
Translation, Introduction & Notes by Paul Smith. 174 pages.

RUBA'IYAT OF ABU SA'ID
Translation, Introduction & Notes by Paul Smith. 227 pages.

RUBA'IYAT OF BABA TAHIR
Translations, Introduction & Notes by Paul Smith. 154 pages.

THE POETS OF SHIRAZ
Sufi, Dervish, Court & Satirical Poets from the 9th to the 20th
Centuries of the fabled City of Shiraz .
Translations & Introduction & Notes by Paul Smith. 428 pages.

RUBA'IYAT OF 'ATTAR
Translation, Introduction & Notes by Paul Smith. 138 Pages.

RUBA'IYAT OF MAHSATI
Translation, Introduction & Notes by Paul Smith. 150 Pages.

RUBA'IYAT OF JAHAN KHATUN
Translation by Paul Smith with Rezvaneh Pashai
Introduction & Notes by Paul Smith. 157 Pages.

RUBA'IYAT OF SANA'I
Translation, Introduction & Notes by Paul Smith. 129 Pages.

RUBA'IYAT OF JAMI
Translation, Introduction & Notes by Paul Smith. 179 Pages.

RUBA'IYAT OF SARMAD
Translation, Introduction & Notes by Paul Smith. 381 pages.

RUBA'IYAT OF HAFIZ
Translation, Introduction & Notes by Paul Smith. 221 Pages.

GREAT SUFI POETS OF THE PUNJAB & SINDH:
AN ANTHOLOGY
Translations & Introductions by Paul Smith 166 pages.

YUNUS EMRE, THE TURKISH DERVISH:
SELECTED POEMS
Translation, Introduction & Notes by Paul Smith. Pages 237.

RUBA'IYAT OF KAMAL AD-DIN
Translation, Introduction & Notes by Paul Smith. Pages 170.

RUBA'YAT OF KHAYYAM
Translation, Introduction & Notes by Paul Smith
Reprint of 1909 Introduction by R.A. Nicholson. 268 pages.

RUBA'IYAT OF AUHAD UD-DIN
Translation and Introduction by Paul Smith. 127 pages.

RUBA'IYAT OF AL-MA'ARRI
Translation & Introduction by Paul Smith. 151 pages

ANTHOLOGY OF CLASSICAL ARABIC POETRY
(From Pre-Islamic Times to Al-Shushtari)
Translations, Introduction and Notes by Paul Smith. Pages 287.

THE QIT'A
Anthology of the 'Fragment' in Arabic, Persian and Eastern Poetry.
Translations, Introduction and Notes by Paul Smith. Pages 423.

HEARTS WITH WINGS
Anthology of Persian Sufi and Dervish Poetry
Translations, Introductions, Etc., by Paul Smith. Pages 623.

HAFIZ: SELECTED POEMS
Translation, Introduction & Notes by Paul Smith. 227 Pages.

'ATTAR: SELECTED POETRY
Translation, Introduction & Notes by Paul Smith. 222 pages.

SANA'I : SELECTED POEMS
Translation, Introduction & Notes by Paul Smith. 148 Pages.

THE ROSE GARDEN OF MYSTERY: SHABISTARI
Translation by Paul Smith.
Introduction by E.H. Whinfield & Paul Smith. Pages 182.

RUDAKI: SELECTED POEMS
Translation, Introduction & Notes by Paul Smith. 142 pages.

SADI: SELECTED POEMS
Translation, Introduction & Notes by Paul Smith. 207 pages.

JAMI: SELECTED POEMS
Translation, Introduction by Paul Smith. 183 Pages.

NIZAMI: SELECTED POEMS
Translation & Introduction by Paul Smith. 235 pages.

RUBA'IYAT OF BEDIL
Translation & Introduction by Paul Smith. 154 pages.

BEDIL: SELECTED POEMS
Translation & Introduction by Paul Smith. Pages... 147.

ANVARI: SELECTED POEMS
Translation & Introduction by Paul Smith. 164 pages.

RUBA'IYAT OF 'IRAQI
Translation & Introduction by Paul Smith. 138 pages.

THE WISDOM OF IBN YAMIN: SELECTED POEMS
Translation & Introduction Paul Smith. 155 pages.

NESIMI: SELECTED POEMS
Translation & Introduction by Paul Smith. 169 pages.

SHAH NI'TMATULLAH: SELECTED POEMS
Translation & Introduction by Paul Smith. 168 pages.

AMIR KHUSRAU: SELECTED POEMS
Translation & Introduction by Paul Smith. 201 pages.

A WEALTH OF POETS:
Persian Poetry at the Courts of Sultan Mahmud in Ghazneh
& Sultan Sanjar in Ganjeh (998-1158)
Translations, Introduction and Notes by Paul Smith. Pages 264.

SHIMMERING JEWELS: Anthology of Poetry Under the Reigns
of the Mughal Emperors of India (1526-1857)
Translations, Introductions, Etc. by Paul Smith. Pages 463.

RAHMAN BABA: SELECTED POEMS
Translation & Introduction by Paul Smith. 141 pages.

RUBA'IYAT OF DARA SHIKOH
Translation & Introduction by Paul Smith. 148 pages.

ANTHOLOGY OF POETRY OF THE CHISHTI SUFI
ORDER Translations & Introduction by Paul Smith. Pages 313.

POEMS OF MAJNUN
Translation & Introduction by Paul Smith. 220 pages.

RUBA'IYAT OF SHAH NI'MATULLAH
Translation & Introduction by Paul Smith. 125 pages.

ANSARI: SELECTED POEMS
Translation & Introduction by Paul Smith. 156 pages.

BABA FARID: SELECTED POEMS
Translation & Introduction by Paul Smith. 164 pages.

POETS OF THE NI'MATULLAH SUFI ORDER
Translations & Introduction by Paul Smith. 244 pages.

MU'IN UD-DIN CHISHTI: SELECTED POEMS
Translation & Introduction by Paul Smith. 171 pages.

QASIDAH BURDAH:
THE THREE POEMS OF THE PROPHET'S MANTLE
Translations & Introduction by Paul Smith. Pages 116.

KHUSHAL KHAN KHATTAK: THE GREAT POET
& WARRIOR OF AFGHANISTAN, SELECTED POEMS
Translation & Introduction by Paul Smith. Pages 187.

RUBA'IYAT OF ANVARI
Translation & Introduction by Paul Smith. 104 pages.

'IRAQI: SELECTED POEMS
Translation & Introduction by Paul Smith. 156 pages.

MANSUR HALLAJ: SELECTED POEMS
Translation & Introduction by Paul Smith. Pages 178.

RUBA'IYAT OF BABA AFZAL
Translation & Introduction by Paul Smith. 178 pages.

RUMI: SELECTIONS FROM HIS *MASNAVI*
Translation & Introduction by Paul Smith. 260 pages.

WINE OF LOVE: AN ANTHOLOGY,
Wine in the Poetry of Arabia, Persia, Turkey &
the Indian Sub-Continent from Pre-Islamic Times to the Present
Translations & Introduction by Paul Smith. 645 pages.

GHALIB: SELECTED POEMS
Translation & Introduction by Paul Smith. Pages 200.

THE ENLIGHTENED SAYINGS OF HAZRAT 'ALI
The Right Hand of the Prophet
Translation & Introduction by Paul Smith. Pages 260.

HAFIZ: TONGUE OF THE HIDDEN
A Selection of *Ghazals* from his *Divan*

Translation & Introduction Paul Smith. 133 pages. Third Edition.

~ HAFIZ: A DAYBOOK ~
Translation & Introduction by Paul Smith. 375 pages.

~* RUMI* ~ A Daybook
Translation & Introduction by Paul Smith. Pages 383.

SUFI POETRY OF INDIA ~ A Daybook~
Translation & Introduction by Paul Smith. Pages 404.

~ SUFI POETRY~ A Daybook
Translation & Introduction by Paul Smith. Pages 390.

~*KABIR*~ A Daybook
Translation & Introduction by Paul Smith. 382 pages.

~ABU SA'ID & SARMAD~ A Sufi Daybook
Translation & Introduction by Paul Smith. 390 pages.

~*SADI*~ A Daybook
Translation & Introduction by Paul Smith. 394 pages.

NIZAMI, KHAYYAM & 'IRAQI ... A Daybook
Translation & Introduction by Paul Smith. 380 pages.

ARABIC & AFGHAN SUFI POETRY ... A Daybook
Translation & Introduction by Paul Smith. 392 pages.

TURKISH & URDU SUFI POETS... A Daybook
Translation & Introduction by Paul Smith. 394 pages.

SUFI & DERVISH RUBA'IYAT (9th – 14th century) A DAYBOOK
Translation & Introduction by Paul Smith. 394 pages.

SUFI & DERVISH RUBA'IYAT (14th[th] – 20th century)
A DAYBOOK

Translation & Introduction by Paul Smith. 394 pages.

~SAYINGS OF THE BUDDHA: A DAYBOOK~
Revised Translation by Paul Smith from F. Max Muller's. 379 pages.

GREAT WOMEN MYSTICAL POETS OF THE EAST
~ A Daybook ~
Translation & Introduction by Paul Smith. 385 pages.

ABU NUWAS SELECTED POEMS
Translation & Introduction by Paul Smith. 154 pages.

HAFIZ: THE SUN OF SHIRAZ:
Essays, Talks, Projects on the Immortal Poet
by Paul Smith. 249 pages.

~*NAZIR AKBARABADI*~ SELECTED POEMS
Translation and Introduction Paul Smith. 191 pages.

~RUBA'IYAT OF IQBAL~
Translation & Introduction by Paul Smith. 175 pages.

~*IQBAL*~ SELECTED POETRY
Translation & Introduction by Paul Smith. 183 pages.

>THE POETRY OF INDIA<
Anthology of Poets of India from 3500 B.C. to the 20th century
Translations, Introductions... Paul Smith. Pages... 622.

BHAKTI POETRY OF INDIA... AN ANTHOLOGY

Translations & Introductions Paul Smith. Pages 236.

SAYINGS OF KRISHNA: A DAYBOOK
Translation & Introduction Paul Smith. Pages 376.

~CLASSIC POETRY OF AZERBAIJAN~ An Anthology~
Translation & Introduction Paul Smith. 231 pages.

THE TAWASIN: MANSUR HALLAJ
(Book of the Purity of the Glory of the One)
Translation & Introduction Paul Smith. Pages 264.

MOHAMMED In Arabic, Sufi & Eastern Poetry
Translation & Introduction by Paul Smith. Pages 245.

GITA GOVINDA
The Dance of Divine Love of Radha & Krishna
>Jayadeva< Translation by Puran Singh & Paul Smith. Pages 107.

GREAT WOMEN MYSTICAL POETS OF THE EAST
~ A Daybook ~
Translation & Introduction by Paul Smith. 385 pages.

~SUFI LOVE POETRY~ An Anthology
Translation & Introduction Paul Smith. Pages 560.

HUMA: SELECTED POEMS OF MEHER BABA
Translation & Introduction Paul Smith. Pages 244.

RIBALD POEMS OF THE SUFI POETS
Abu Nuwas, Sana'i, Anvari, Mahsati, Rumi, Sadi and Obeyd Zakani
... Translation & Introduction Paul Smith. 206 pages.

FIVE GREAT EARLY SUFI MASTER POETS
Mansur Hallaj, Baba Tahir, Abu Sa'id, Ansari & Sana'i
Translation & Introduction by Paul Smith. Pages 617

FIVE GREAT CLASSIC SUFI MASTER POETS
Khaqani, Mu'in ud-din Chishti, 'Attar & Auhad ud-din Kermani
Translation & Introduction Paul Smith. Pages 541.

ANTHOLOGY OF WOMEN MYSTICAL POETS
OF THE MIDDLE-EAST & INDIA
Translation & Introduction Paul Smith. Pages 497.

FOUR MORE GREAT CLASSIC SUFI MASTER POETS
Sadi, 'Iraqi, Yunus Emre, Shabistari.
Translation & Introduction Paul Smith. Pages 562.

~ANOTHER~
FOUR GREAT CLASSIC SUFI MASTER POETS
Amir Khusrau, Ibn Yamin, Hafiz & Nesimi
Translation & Introduction Paul Smith. Pages 636.

FOUR GREAT LATER CLASSIC SUFI MASTER POETS
Shah Ni'mat'ullah, Jami, Dara Shikoh & Makhfi
Translation & Introduction Paul Smith. Pages 526.

THE FOUR LAST GREAT SUFI MASTER POETS
Shah Latif, Nazir Akbarabadi, Ghalib and Iqbal
Translation & Introduction Paul Smith. Pages 616.

'ATTAR & KHAQANI: SUFI POETRY ~A Daybook~
Translation & Introduction Paul Smith. 388 pages.

POET-SAINTS OF MAHARASHTRA:
SELECTED POEMS
Translations & Introductions by Paul Smith. Pages 198.

ABHANGS & BHAJANS OF THE GREATEST INDIAN
POET-SAINTS
Translations & Introductions Paul Smith. Pages 214.

A TREASURY OF LESSER-KNOWN GREAT SUFI POETS
Translation & Introduction Paul Smith. Pages 736.

HATEF OF ISFAHAN AND HIS FAMOUS TARJI-BAND
Translation & Introduction Paul Smith. Pages 129.

CLASSIC BATTLE POEMS OF ANCIENT INDIA
& ARABIA, PERSIA & AFGHANISTAN
Translation & Introduction Paul Smith. Pages 246.

Large Format Paperback, 7″ x 10″ Illustrated 183 pages

HAFEZ: THE DIVAN
Volume One: The Poems
Revised Translation Paul Smith
Large Format Paperback "7 x 10" 578 pages

HAFEZ: THE DIVAN
Volume Two: Introduction
Paul Smith
Large Format Paperback 7″ x 10″ 224 pages.

~ SAADI ~ THE DIVAN
Revised Translation & Introduction Paul Smith
Large Format Paperback 7″ x 10″ 548 pages.

HAFEZ: BOOK OF DIVINATION
Translation, Introduction & Interpretations by Paul Smith
Large Format Edition, 7″ x 10″ 441 pages

LAYLA AND MAJNUN: NIZAMI
Translation & Introduction by Paul Smith
Large Format Edition, 7″ x 10″ 239 pages.

HAFEZ: DIVAN
Revised Translation, Introduction Etc by Paul Smith
Large Format Edition 7″ x 10″ 800 pages.

HAFEZ OF SHIRAZ:
The Life, Poetry and Times of the Immortal Persian Poet
Books 1.2 & 3. (The Early Years, The Middle Years, The Later Years)
by Paul Smith
Large Format Edition 7″ x 10″ over 800 pages each book.

OMAR KHAYYAM: RUBA'IYAT
Translation & Introduction Paul Smith
Reprint of 1909 Introduction by R.A. Nicholson
Large Format Edition, 7″ x 10″ Illustrated, 280 pages.

ROSE GARDEN OF MYSTERY: SHABISTARI
Translation by Paul Smith.
Introduction by E.H. Whinfield & Paul Smith
Large Format Edition 7" x 10" 182 pages.

SUFIS, PRINCESSES & DERVISHES, MARTYRS &
FEMINISTS: Ten Great Women Poets of the East
Translations & Introductions Paul Smith
Large Format Edition 7" x 10" 410 pages.

ARABIC SUFI POETRY: An Anthology
Translation & Introduction Paul Smith
Large Format Edition 7" x 10" 387 pages.

A QUILT OF WOMEN SPIRITUAL POETS OF THE
MIDDLE-EAST & INDIA
Translation & Introduction Paul Smith
Large Format Edition 7" x 10" 509 pages.

THE BOOK OF ABU SA'ID
Ruba'iyat... Life & Times & Teachings
Translation by Paul Smith
Introduction by Paul Smith & R.A. Nicholson
Large Format Edition 7" x 10" 350 pages.

THE BOOK OF KABIR
Short Poems *[Sakhis]*
Translation & Introduction Paul Smith
Large Format Edition 7" x 10" 698 pages.

~RUMI~ *Ruba'iyat*
Translation & Introduction Paul Smith
Large Format Edition 7" x 10" 368 pages

THE BOOK OF FARID AL-DIN 'ATTAR
Ruba'is, Ghazals & Masnavis
Translation & Introduction Paul Smith

Large Format Edition 7″ x 10″ 207 pages

THE BOOK OF OBEYD ZAKANI
Poetry, Prose, Satire, Jokes and Ribaldry.
Translation and Introduction by Paul Smith
Large Format Edition 7″ x 10″ 357 pages.

THE BOOK OF MANSUR HALLAJ
Selected Poems & The Tawasin
Translation & Introduction Paul Smith
Large Format Edition 7″ x 10″ 323 pages

THE BOOK OF RUMI
Ruba'is, Ghazals, Masnavis and a *Qasida*
Translation & Introduction Paul Smith
Large Format Edition 7″ x 10″ 476 pages.

THE BOOK OF SARMAD
Translation & Introduction Paul Smith
Large Format Edition 7″ x 10″ 407 pages

THE BOOK OF IBN AL-FARID
Translation & Introduction Paul Smith
Large Format Edition 7″ x 10″ 178 pages

THREE SUFI-MARTYR POETS OF INDIA
Sarmad, Dara Shikoh & Makhfi
Translation & Introduction Paul Smith
Large Format Edition 7″ x 10″ pages 334.

THE BOOK OF KHAQANI
Translation & Introduction by Paul Smith
Large Format Paperback 7′ x 10″ pages 230

DRUNK ON GOD
Anthology Poems by God-Realized & God-Intoxicated Poets
Translation & Introduction by Paul Smith
Large Format Paperback 7″ x 10″ pages 804.

POETRY OF INDIA
Anthology of the Greatest Poets of India
Translations, Introductions by Paul Smith
Large Format Paperback 7″ x 10″ Pages 760

THE BOOK OF JAMI
Translation & Introduction by Paul Smith
Large Format Paperback 7″ x 10″ pages 233.

THE BOOK OF ANSARI
Translation & Introduction by Paul Smith
Large Format Paperback 7″ x 10″ pages 231.

YUNUS EMRE & NESIMI:
THE TWO GREAT TURKISH SUFI POETS...
Their Lives & a Selection of their Poems
Translation & Introduction Paul Smith
Large Format Paperback 7″ x 10″ 416 pages.

THE BOOK OF NESIMI
Translation & Introduction by Paul Smith
Large Format Paperback 7″ x 10″ pages 250.

THE BOOK OF IQBAL
Translation & Introduction by Paul Smith
Large Format Paperback 7″ x 10″ pages 252.

THE BOOK OF 'IRAQI
Translation & Introduction by Paul Smith
Large Format Paperback 7″ x 10″ pages 186.

THE BOOK OF TURKISH POETRY
Anthology of Sufi, Dervish, Divan, Court & Folk Poetry
from the 12th – 20th Century
Translation & Introduction Paul Smith
7″ x 10″ Large Format Paperback 341 pages

THE BOOK OF HAFIZ (HAFEZ)
Translation, Introduction Etc. Paul Smith
Large Format Edition 7″ x 10″ 532 pages.

THE BOOK OF SANA'I
Translation & Introduction Paul Smith
Large Format Paperback 167 pages.

THE BOOK OF ECSTASY OR
THE BALL & THE POLO-STICK
by 'Arifi
Translation & Introduction Paul Smith
Large Format Paperback 7″ x 10″ 221 pages.

ANTHOLOGY OF SUFI & FOLK STROPHE POEMS
OF PERSIA AND THE INDIAN SUB-CONTINENT
Translation & Introduction Paul Smith
Large Format Paperback 7″ x 10″ 423 pages.

THE BOOK OF MAJNUN
Translation & Introduction by Paul Smith
Large Format Paperback 7″ x 10″ 336 pages.

THE BOOK OF MU'IN UD-DIN CHISHTI
Translation & Introduction Paul Smith
Large Format Paperback 7″ x 10″ 315 pages.

THE BOOK OF SHAH NI'MAT'ULLAH
Translation & Introduction Paul Smith
Large Format Paperback 7″ x 10″ 232 pages.

THE BOOK OF NAZIR AKBARABADI
Translation & Introduction Paul Smith
Large Format Paperback 7″ x 10″ 329 pages.

POETS OF SHIRAZ AT THE TIME OF HAFIZ
Translation & Introduction Paul Smith 455 pages.

THE BIG BOOK OF SUFI POETRY
An Anthology
Translation & Introduction by Paul Smith
Large Format 7" x 10" 798 pages.

THE BIG BOOK OF PERSIAN POETRY: An Anthology
Court, Sufi, Dervish, Satirical, Ribald, Prison and Social Poetry
from the 9th to the 20th century
Translation, Introduction by Paul Smith
Large Format Paperback 7" x 10" 777 pages

THE BOOK OF SHABISTARI
The Rose Garden of Mystery
Translation & Introduction Paul Smith
Large Format Paperback 7" x 10" 261 pages.

THE BOOK OF ABU NUWAS
Translation & Introduction Paul Smith
Large Format Paperback 7" x 10" 196 pages.

THE BOOK OF DARA SHIKOH
Life, Poems & Prose
Large Format Paperback 7" x 10" 276 pages.

BHAGAVAD GITA & GITA GOVINDA
Translation & Introduction Paul Smith
With Shri Purohit Swami & Puran Singh
Large Format Paperback 7" x 10" 360 pages.

THE BOOK OF AMIR KHUSRAU
Translation & Introduction Paul Smith
Large Format Paperback 7" x 10" 441 pages

THE BOOK OF YUNUS EMRE
Translation & Introduction Paul Smith
Large Format Paperback 7" x 10" 253 pages

THE BOOK OF BABA TAHIR ORYAN
Translation & Introduction Paul Smith
Large Format Paperback 7" x 10" 187 pages

THE BOOK OF GHALIB
Translation & Introduction Paul Smith
Large Format Paperback 7" x 10" 194 pages

THE *RUBA'I* (QUATRAIN) IN SUFI POETRY
An Anthology
Translation & Introduction Paul Smith
Large Format Paperback 7" x 10" 450 pages

THE BOOK OF AL-MA'ARRI
Translation & Introduction Paul Smith
Large Format Paperback 7" x 10" 172 pages

THE BOOK OF ANVARI
Translation & Introduction Paul Smith
Large Format Paperback 7" x 10" 168 pages

THE BOOK OF KAMAL AL-DIN ISFAHANI
Translation & Introduction Paul Smith
Large Format Paperback 7" x 10" 170 pages

THE BOOK OF ABDUL-QADER BEDIL
Translation & Introduction Paul Smith
Large Format Paperback 7" x 10" 173 pages

THE BOOK OF BABA AFDAL KASHINI
Translation & Introduction Paul Smith
Large Format Paperback 7" x 10" 173 pages

THE BOOK OF ANSARI
Translation & Introduction Paul Smith
Large Format Paperback 7" x 10" 236 pages

THE BOOK OF KHUSHAL KHAN
Translation & Introduction by Paul Smith
Large Format Paperback 7" x 10" 189 pages.

THE BOOK OF RAHMAN BABA
Translation & Introduction by Paul Smith
Large Format Paperback 7" x 10" 186 pages.

THE BOOK OF BULLEH SHAH
Translation & Introduction by Paul Smith
Large Format Paperback 7" x 10" 193 pages

THE BOOK OF MAHSATI GANJAVI
Translation & Introduction by Paul Smith
Large Format Paperback 7" x 10" 182 pages.

THE BOOK OF IBN YAMIN
Translation & Introduction by Paul Smith
Large Format Paperback 7" x 10" 207 pages.

THE BOOK OF HUMA
The Poems of Meher Baba
Translation & Introduction by Paul Smith
Large Format Paperback 7" x 10" 332 pages.

~Introduction to Sufi Poets Series~

Life & Poems of the following Sufi poets, Translations &
Introductions: Paul Smith

'AISHAH AI-BA'UNIYAH, AMIR KHUSRAU, ANSARI,
ANVARI, AL-MA'ARRI, 'ATTAR, ABU SA'ID, AUHAD UD-
DIN, BABA FARID, BABA AZFAL, BABA TAHIR, BEDIL,
BULLEH SHAH, DARA SHIKOH, GHALIB, HAFIZ, IBN
'ARABI, IBN YAMIN, IBN AL-FARID, IQBAL, INAYAT
KHAN, 'IRAQI, JAHAN KHATUN, JAMI, KAMAL AD-
DIN, KABIR, KHAQANI, KHAYYAM, LALLA DED,

MAKHFI, MANSUR HALLAJ, MU'IN UD-DIN CHISHTI,
NAZIR AKBARABADI, NESIMI, NIZAMI, OBEYD
ZAKANI, RAHMAN BABA, RUMI, SANA'I, SADI,
SARMAD, SHABISTARI, SHAH LATIF, SHAH
NI'MAT'ULLAH, SULTAN BAHU, YUNUS EMRE, EARLY
ARABIC SUFI POETS, EARLY PERSIAN SUFI POETS,
URDU SUFI POETS, TURKISH SUFI POETS, AFGHAN
SUFI POETS 90 pages each.

POETRY

THE MASTER, THE MUSE & THE POET
An Autobiography in Poetry
by Paul Smith. 654 Pages.

~A BIRD IN HIS HAND~
POEMS FOR AVATAR MEHER BABA
by Paul Smith. 424 pages.

PUNE: THE CITY OF GOD
(A Spiritual Guidebook to the New Bethlehem)
Poems & Photographs in Praise of Avatar Meher Baba
by Paul Smith. 159 pages.

COMPASSIONATE ROSE
Recent *Ghazals* for Avatar Meher Baba
by Paul Smith. 88 pages.

~THE ULTIMATE PIRATE~
(and the Shanghai of Imagination)
A FABLE by Paul Smith. 157 pages.

+THE CROSS OF GOD+
A Poem in the *Masnavi* Form
by Paul Smith (7 x 10 inches)

RUBA'IYAT ~ of ~ PAUL SMITH
Pages 236.

SONG OF SHINING WONDER
& OTHER *MASNAVI* POEMS
Paul Smith. Pages 171.

~TEAMAKER'S *DIVAN... GHAZALS*~
Paul Smith. Pages 390.

CRADLE MOUNTAIN
Paul Smith... Illustrations – John Adam.
(7x10 inches) Second Edition.

~BELOVED & LOVER~
Ghazals by Paul Smith... inspired by Meher Baba
Pages 410.

POEMS INSPIRED BY 'GOD SPEAKS' BY MEHER BABA
Paul Smith... Pages 168.

MEHER BABA'S SECLUSION HILL
Poems & Photographs by Paul Smith
"7 x 10" 120 pages.

~DIVAN~ *Ghazals...* 1974 - 2014
Paul Smith. Pages 740

A BOOK OF QUATRAINS FOR THE ONE
by Paul Smith
Large Format 7" x 10" 511 pages.

FICTION

THE FIRST MYSTERY A Novel of the Road...
by Paul Smith. 541 pages. Large Format Edition 589 pages

~THE HEALER AND THE EMPEROR~
A Historical Novel Based on a True Story
by Paul Smith Pages 149.

>>>GOING<<<BACK...
A Novel by Paul Smith. 164 pages.

THE GREATEST GAME
A Romantic Comedy Adventure With A Kick!
by Paul Smith 187 pages.

GOLF IS MURDER! A Miles Driver Golfing Mystery
by Paul Smith. 176 pages.

THE ZEN-GOLF MURDER!
A Miles Driver Golfing Mystery
by Paul Smith 146 pages.

~RIANA~ A Novel
by Paul Smith 154 pages.

CHILDREN'S FICTION

PAN OF THE NEVER-NEVER
by Paul Smith 167 pages.

~HAFIZ~
The Ugly Little Boy who became a Great Poet
by Paul Smith 195 pages.

SCREENPLAYS

>>>GOING<<<BACK...
A Movie of War & Peace Based on a True Story ...
Screenplay by Paul Smith

HAFIZ OF SHIRAZ
The Life, Poetry and Times of the Immortal Persian Poet.
A Screenplay by Paul Smith

LAYLA & MAJNUN BY NIZAMI
A Screenplay by Paul Smith

PAN OF THE NEVER-NEVER...
A Screenplay by Paul Smith

THE GREATEST GAME
A Romantic Comedy Adventure With A Kick!
A Screenplay
by Paul Smith

GOLF IS MURDER!
Screenplay
by Paul Smith

THE HEALER & THE EMPEROR
A True Story... Screenplay
by Paul Smith

THE * KISS ... A Screen-Play
by Paul Smith

THE ZEN-GOLF MURDER!
A Screenplay by Paul Smith

TELEVISION

HAFIZ OF SHIRAZ:
A Television Series
by Paul Smith

THE FIRST MYSTERY
A Television Series For The New Humanity
by Paul Smith

THE MARK: The Australian Game
A Thirteen-Part Doco-Drama for Television
by Paul Smith

PLAYS, MUSICALS

HAFIZ: THE MUSICAL DRAMA
by Paul Smith

THE SINGER OF SHIRAZ
A Radio Musical-Drama on the Life of Persia's Immortal Poet,
Hafiz of Shiraz by Paul Smith

MEMOIR

SLIPPING THROUGH THE CRACKS
A Memoir by Ron Roberts 186 pages

ART

MY DOGS
From the Sketchbooks of Gus Cohen.   8" x 10" 224 pages

A BRIDGE TO THE MASTER ... MEHER BABA
Paintings & Drawings, Poems & Essays
by Oswald Hall
Edited & Introduction by Paul Smith   8" x 10" 337 pages.

MY VIEW From the Sketchbooks of Gus Cohen,
Barkers Creek Castlemaine 8" x 10" 210 pages.

THE ART OF KEVIN SMITH
Paintings & Drawings, Sculpture, Furniture,
Mirrors, Boxes & Photographs
8" x 10" 337 pages full colour

"To penetrate into the essence of all being and significance
and to release the fragrance of that inner attainment
for the guidance and benefit of others, by expressing
in the world of forms, truth, love, purity and beauty...
this is the only game which has any intrinsic and absolute
worth. All other, happenings, incidents and attainments can,
in themselves, have no lasting importance."

Meher Baba

CPSIA information can be obtained
at www.ICGtesting.com
Printed in the USA
LVHW061454100123
736819LV00011B/1083

9 781508 472612